Joe Stahlkuppe

Keeshonden

Everything About Purchase, Care, Nutrition,
Breeding, Behavior and Training

With illustrations by Michele Earle-Bridges
and 31 Color Photos

Consulting Editor: Matthew M. Vriends, Ph.D.

BARRON'S

Photo Credits:
Gary W. Ellis: pages 9 (bottom left and right), 63 (top left), back cover (bottom right); Michele Earle-Bridges: front cover, pages 9 (top right), 10 (top right and bottom), 45, 46, 63 (top right), back cover (top left and right); Robin Stark: pages 27, 28 (bottom); Judith E. Strom: pages 9 (top left), 10 (top left), 28 (top left and right), 63 (bottom left), back cover (bottom left); Wim van Vught: inside front cover, page 64; B. Everett Webb: page 63 (bottom right), inside back cover.

All inquiries should be addressed to:
Barron's Educational Series, Inc.
250 Wireless Boulevard
Hauppauge, New York 11788

Library of Congress Catalog Card No. 93-10734

International Standard Book No. 0-8120-1560-6

Library of Congress Cataloging-in-Publication Data

Stahlkuppe, Joe.
    Keeshonden : everything about purchase, care, nutrition, breeding, behavior, and training / Joe Stahlkuppe ; with illustrations by Michele Earle-Bridges ; consulting editor, Matthew M. Vriends.
        p.   cm.—(A Complete pet owner's manual)
    Includes bibliographical references (p.   ) and index. ISBN: 0-8120-1560-6
    1. Keeshonds.   I. Vriends, Matthew M.
    II. Title.   III. Series.
    SF429.K4S73   1993
    636.7'2—dc20   93-10734
                                                     CIP

About the Author: Joe Stahlkuppe, who writes a column for a pet industry magazine, is a lifelong dog fancier and breeder. Employed as a regional sales director for a major pet food manufacturer, he is also the author of Barron's *Pomeranians, a Complete Pet Owner's Manual*.

Advice and Warning: This book is concerned with buying, keeping, and raising Keeshonden. The publisher and the author think it is important to point out that the advice and information for Keeshond maintenance applies to healthy, normally developed animals. Anyone who buys an adult Keeshond or one from an animal shelter must consider that the animal may have behavioral problems and may, for example, bite without any visible provocation. Such anxiety-biters are dangerous for the owner as well as for the general public.

Caution is further advised in the association of children with a Keeshond, in meetings with other dogs, and in exercising the dog without a leash.

PRINTED IN HONG KONG
56   9927   0987654

Contents

Contents

Foreword

"Necessity is the mother of invention." Most breeds of dogs have been developed to meet a specific need. Because of different circumstances, the needs varied, and individual breeds answered different human problems, often quite specifically. A sled dog, for example, would usually be a poor hunting dog. Conversely, most hunting dogs could not endure the harshness of pulling a sled full time. Usually, even though a dog might be able to do several things passably, one skill was extraordinary.

The Keeshond is an exception to this rule. This charming, elegant clown of a dog is one of the true generalists of the canine world. Always a companion, it has served to pull a cart, guard a barge, and even to hunt. But the main role of the Keeshond, formerly and now, is as a friend and partner — a broadly defined job in which the Kees has excelled.

That the Keeshond is around at all is amazing. The victim of political fallout that left it a symbol of treason, lacking a specific task to draw dog fanciers from other lands, saddled with a difficult name, a lesser breed would have fallen into the abyss of breeds that once were. But there is something of the persistence of the Dutch people in the Keeshond. It is therefore not surprising that a people who have wrested fertile farmland from the bottom of the sea would also produce a breed that could overcome almost any obstacle.

Many thanks to the Keeshonden people who take such pride in their favorite breed. Numerous Kees breeders and exhibitors have taken time to offer advice and share stories about a wonderful breed. Their code of ethics is a model that fanciers of other canines would do well to follow, especially to avoid the pitfalls of popularity that

have ensnared some other breeds. Special among these people are Robin Stark (a Renaissance person of rare ability) and Kees fan and breeder, Brenda Whitaker.

High regard and gratitude go to some very special people. Much love and many thanks to my wife Cathie, my son Shawn, and his wife Lisa for their support in the completion of this book. My sincerest appreciation to the great folks at Barron's, especially senior editor, Don Reis, and to Michele Earle-Bridges, an artist who loves dogs and whose work reflects it! I would also like to thank Petra Burgmann, DVM and Helgard Niewisch, DVM, both of whom read the manuscript and made constructive suggestions.

This book has a threefold dedication: (1) to my dad, Gerald E. Stahlkuppe, Sr. who fostered in me a love for dogs, but who did not live to see this book completed; (2) to my father-in-law and mother-in-law, B.K. and Bennie McDonald, whose love and kind understanding means so much; (3) to my good friend and consulting editor, Dr. Matthew M. Vriends. Like the Keeshond, he is a product of the Netherlands who has gained a multitude of friends the world over!

Great admiration goes to the Keeshonden themselves. When one has to struggle to discover the negatives about a breed, that breed is special. The Keeshond, throughout its long association with humankind, has not been acclaimed for hunting, herding, sledding, working, or racing. The Keeshond has been largely relegated to the role of companion. Knowing the breed, I believe this stalwart little Dutch dog wouldn't have it any other way!

Understanding the Keeshond

Popular breeds of dogs require no introduction to would-be owners. Generally, people have some idea about a breed before they consider it as a canine member of the family. The Keeshond, however, appears to be an exception to this rule; therefore, introductions are in order.

To begin with, the Keeshond has a name that is not pronounced as it looks. The correct pronunciation is "Kayz-hawnd" (*never* "keys-hound"). Two or more members of this breed are referred to as "Keeshonden" (not "Keeshonds"). The name and the "en" plural ending, like the breed itself, trace back to Dutch ancestry.

To compound the confusion, the Keeshond has been assigned by several national kennel clubs to that interesting, but rather disconnected grouping known as the "Nonsporting Breeds." In the United States, this canine catchall category has such worthies as the bulldog, the dalmatian, the Boston terrier and several others. Not specifically hunters, herders, or working dogs, these breeds, including the Kees, seem to specialize as pets.

Indeed, the Keeshond's long and close affiliation with humans has made it an excellent companion. Unlike other breeds that owe their beginnings to an individual breeder or to a specific sport or chore, the Keeshond was discovered and refined by the early Netherlanders. Today it remains what it has always been — "a people dog." Though the early Dutch found in the forebears of the Keeshond the rudimentary ability to work, herd, or even hunt, it was not for this diverse potential that they valued the ancestors of the breed. It was for the Kees' manifest capacity as companions and friends that these sturdy spitz became a favorite of ordinary working folk.

Early History of the Keeshond

Fossil findings excavated from a number of Swiss lakes have identified a dog quite similar to the Keeshond of today. Keeslike dogs have been portrayed in the art of many cultures throughout

The Keeshond, a sturdy silver-gray spitz breed from the Netherlands, shows the characteristic "spectacles" around its eyes and an impressive mane of long hair around its neck.

recorded history. Proponents of other spitz breeds may claim these portrayals attest to the age of their specific breed. Nevertheless, a simple fact remains: many of these ancient paintings, sculptures, and vase decorations closely resemble the Keeshond. In fact, these artistic representations more closely resemble the modern Kees and its breed cousins, the Pomeranian, the Norwegian elkhound, and the Finnish spitz than any others. Dutch researchers believe these early dogs from what would become Switzerland migrated over the centuries with their human companions. Utilizing rafts and barges early pre-Europeans probably traveled down the Rhine River to settle what is now the Netherlands. The future Keeshonden are thought to have accompanied the future Dutch people as guards, watchdogs, and companions.

The next evidence of the rich history of the Keeshond is also an artistic representation. During the Middle Ages, a dog, undeniably of Keeshond type, appeared on the seal of the city of Amsterdam. The scene depicted on this seal is the founding of the capital of the Netherlands, one of the world's great cities.

The Keeshond's role in Dutch history did not end with the founding of Amsterdam. During the turmoil of the French Revolution, which rocked most of Europe, the Keeshond became a symbol of the common Netherlanders—the patriots. This spritely spitz, which appeared in the graffiti and political cartoons of the day, was strongly identified with the nationalists who clashed with the supporters of the royal House of Orange.

The leader of the patriots, one Cornelis (or Cornelius) de Ghyselaer, was commonly referred to by his nickname, Kees. De Ghyselaer owned one of the spitz dogs so popular with the people of the Netherlands, and the patriot leader went about his political activities with his dog. The members of de Ghyselaer's political party were called *Kezen* (plural for Kees.) In Dutch, the word *hond* means dog, so the name Keeshond may derive from Keesdog—the pet of Cornelis "Kees" de Ghyselaer and later the pet of the people.

So closely aligned with the patriotic movement was the Keeshond that when de Ghyselaer was executed and his patriots routed, the breed also became politically unpopular. To own a Keeshond at this time was considered almost an admission of patriotic sympathies—an act that could easily have had fatal repercussions. Out of favor with the ruling family of the Netherlands, the Keeshond became a symbol of a failed cause and many dogs of this breed were killed. These were desperate times for the Keeshond. Facing extinction, the Keeshond fell back on the love of the ordinary country people to keep it alive as a breed.

Throughout the breed's history in the Netherlands, the Keeshond was identified first with farms, and later with boats and barges. The Kees became a type of waterborne good luck charm for boatmen and bargemen. A barge would seem incomplete without a "Dutch barge dog" (as the early Keeshonden were often called). Watching over the cargo and living close to the bargemen's families was in keeping with the companion role that was (and is) exemplified by this sturdy spitz of the Netherlands.

Modern History of the Keeshond

As a breed type, the Keeshond is very old; as an officially recognized, registered breed, it is relatively new. For reasons unclear, but perhaps stemming from the political misfortunes of the Keeshond, this great companion and pet was unrecognized by the world of purebred dogs. Close relatives like the Norwegian elkhound, the Samoyed, and even the Kees' little brother, the Pomeranian, all made their debuts in the show ring long before the Keeshond.

When the Keeshond did at last receive some recognition, it was under an incorrect, mildly insulting, and misleading name. In the last quarter of the nineteenth century, Keeshonden were known in England as "The Overweight Pomeranian." The Keeshond was also at various times referred to as "the wolf dog," "the fox dog,"—and, of course, as the "Dutch barge dog."

Like its close kin, the Pomeranian, the Keeshond was indebted to England for bringing it to the attention of dog fanciers, first in Britain and then around the world. Thanks to the efforts of a young British girl, the Keeshond was at last noticed and accepted. While vacationing with her parents in the Netherlands in 1905, Miss Gwendolyn Hamilton-Fletcher, though then still in her teens, was captivated by the attractive dogs of the Dutch bargemen. She brought two shaded gray pups home with her to England and in so doing introduced the breed to the rest of the world.

Miss Hamilton-Fletcher provided an introduction for the people's dog of the Netherlands to the peerage of England. Later as Mrs. Wingfield-Digby, this rehabilitator of the Keeshond imported other dogs from the Netherlands, and through her efforts the breed was accepted for registration by the Kennel Club of England in 1925 as the "Dutch barge dog." Shortly afterward, what may be the most mispronounced of all breed names was officially accepted—and the Keeshond was launched!

Understanding the Keeshond

Perhaps influenced by the awakening of interest in England, the Dutch Keeshond Club had been established in 1924. Ironically, the German spitz, a quite similar and closely related breed, had had a breed registry and breed club even before the turn of the century. Thus the Keeshond, first acknowledged as early as the thirteenth century, finally achieved official recognition six hundred years later!

The first Keeshonden were registered in the United States in 1930 by the American Kennel Club. The breed was quickly accepted, and the people's dog of the Netherlands was transformed within a short span of years from a working, unpedigreed Dutch pet to a registered and titled show dog. According to Keeshond fanciers, the best thing about this rapid ascension, when it finally did occur, was that international acceptance did not come at the cost of those very qualities that had made this dog a good canine companion. The Keeshond, unlike some other great breeds, was not robbed of its native heritage of sound temperament and practical design by generations of show-dog breeding whims. The Keeshond, who began to win hearts in the New World, was for all intents and purposes the same spitz dog that had become the common person's mascot centuries before.

One change that did take place involving the Keeshond was a selection process that left the beautiful shaded silver, wolf-spitz color as the only acceptable standard color in England and later in the United States. In the Netherlands, Keeshonden for generations had come in several colors — white, black, orange-shaded white, and the silver gray. It is this last color that has given the Keeshonden of today their distinctive shaded silver patterns.

Happily, generations of shaded-silver breeding have not resulted in the stamped-out-of-a-pattern uniformity that has occurred in other breeds. While a casual observer might assume that all Kees look alike, close comparison of several dogs will show that the Keeshond, while staying within the prescribed limits of the Standard, often vary subtly. As one breeder put it, Keeshonden can be as different in color as "a room full of gray-haired people." The Kees color can thus range from light silver to dark silver and all shades in between.

One color attribute that remains constant in all properly colored Kees is the dark markings around the eyes. These charming, raccoon-like "spectacles" give the breed a mischievous, happy look.

Characteristic Kees Behavior

Balance is a key word in discussing the Keeshond. Not only is the dog physically well-balanced, Keeshonden are well-balanced emotionally and mentally. While the Kees is a dog of even disposition, keen intelligence, with an active, useful physique, it is as a total package that the Keeshond ranks high on any breed list. This combination of brains and good temperament, wrapped attractively in a shaded-silver package, has made the Kees the companion it is today.

The Kees has a marked desire to please its humans. This desire has done much to make the Kees a good obedience dog. So amenable to proper training is this bright, sturdy dog that Keeshonden have been successfully trained to serve as guide dogs for the blind. Only their lack of size prevented them from being more widely used in this role.

Like most of the spitz family, the Keeshond is a hardy, cheerful dog with a "can do" attitude. Keeshonden are protective of their owners without the aggressiveness that often makes some breeds

The versatile Keeshond is a stylish escort, a rough-and-tumble playmate, a good early-warning watchdog, and, perhaps most of all, a faithful friend and pet.

difficult to predict or manage. Keeshonden make better house watchdogs than house guard dogs because of their seemingly instinctive liking for humans. While a Keeshond might fight to protect its owner, it is not aggressive with neighbors, friends, or even with strangers. The likeable Keeshond will alert its family to visitors, but should not be thought of as a "silver bullet" of protection.

Like other northern breeds, the Keeshonden have a strong attachment to their own "belongings" and their own places. This greatly aids in crate-training and in the socialization of a Kees puppy. Keeshond behavior toward what it considers its own, including its humans, can accurately be described as proprietary.

Keeshond Mental Ability

The Keeshond is a very bright dog as is evidenced by its level of achievement in obedience work. This intelligence makes a Keeshond a good choice for the dog owner who is willing to help a dog learn the right lessons, but also entails added responsibility. Keeshond ownership, when the dog and the human have worked together to become a good pet and a good pet owner, is a very positive experience.

The intelligence of the Keeshond has been widely acknowledged among dog fanciers. Keeshond breeders and owners note that this keen intelligence is both the breed's greatest attribute and biggest potential problem. As one Kees supporter said, "To get the best out of a really smart dog requires a really smart owner."

Breed advocates are quick to share instances that illustrate the mental capacity of the

Regular brushing of a Keeshond's thick coat is usually enough to keep the dog looking good. The dog's feet and toenails will also benefit from consistent care. Good dental care not only helps prevent tooth and gum problems but will keep the Keeshond's breath pleasant.

Keeshond. One amazing account, verified by several people, was of an older Kees that apparently had lost its hearing over a period of time. The dog's owner, a skillful dog trainer and longtime Keeshond breeder, noticed the hearing loss only after observing the dog's complete lack of response to commands when it was not facing her. When the dog turned and could see commands given, it immediately and obediently did what it was told. A medical examination revealed that this Keeshond was completely deaf and had quite possibly learned to read its owner's lips!

Keeshond experts stress consistency and fairness when working with a Kees. "Most dogs, but especially Keeshonden, need and like structure in their environment." One breeder suggested, "With a Keeshond, it would be wise to treat the dog like a very young child. You can expect some resentment from this bright dog if it is treated in an unfair or inconsistent manner."

One breeder stated that even in her obedience work with Keeshonden, the breed's intelligence could sometimes almost be a liability. "Kees do very well in obedience work with trainers who aren't as repetitive as they could be with some other breeds." Evidently the question, "I've mastered this command; why should I do this over and over?" occurs to some Keeshonden.

Kees owners also need to be consistent with their dog's schedule. According to many Keeshond breeders, these dogs almost seem to come equipped with a watch. If Saturday morning is the regular time for Frisbee tossing in the park, many Kees actually come to expect this activity at this time. Breeders say that the dog might accept Friday afternoon, but to wait until Sunday could cause some Keeshonden to fret and perhaps even come up with some minor misdeed as a retaliation. As stated, bright dogs bring added pleasure, but also added responsibility.

A number of Kees people point out that while correction for mistakes or misbehavior is best done with the Keeshond (and all other dogs) at the time of the act, Keeshonden seem to actually remember their sins. One Kees jumped up on a couch when its owner was out of the room, an act it knew was forbidden. The owner saw the dog's misdeed and was about to correct the Kees when a phone call interrupted. A long conversation ensued. When the Kees owner ended the call and remembered the dog on the couch, she went into the living room to find the dog in its crate, acting just as if it had already been punished!

When some human action or inaction seems to bother an intelligent Keeshond, some trainers suggest shifting the dog's concentration by giving it a new toy. Changing the dog's focus can avoid the Kees all-too-human trait of wanting to get even.

One important thing to keep in mind about the Kees is that this is one breed that cannot just be placed in the backyard and fed once a day. The Kees needs to share its owner's home not because it cannot tolerate the elements, but because it must have the stimulation of human interaction. The Kees would, therefore be a great dog for a large family.

Keeshonden and Vocal Expression

There are longtime breeders and fans of the Keeshond who believe the breed can almost talk. So consistent is some Kees' use of little barks, whines, and other sounds that there may be some truth in this assertion. There are many breeder stories about Keeshonden that have been able to develop a type of code of yips and barks that their owners have come to recognize as meaning different things.

The Kees is a great early warning alert dog. After centuries of performing this function in the Netherlands, it remains the only real job the modern Keeshond usually does. The long valued alertness and intelligence of the breed, exceptional hearing and eyesight, and extraordinary scenting ability makes the Keeshond a keen canine sensor. Very little takes place in the Kees' domain that this spritely dog doesn't know about and share with its owner.

As a bright dog, the Keeshond will need training to help it know what needs to be announced with a bark and what doesn't. One owner of an as-yet-untrained Kees puppy told of being alerted to the menace of butterflies and other flying creatures within the airspace of the pup's backyard. Patient training helped this young Keeshond learn that these flying things represented no danger to its household and therefore required no alarm.

The Sensory Organs

As with most of the spitz family, the Keeshond possesses prominent eyes and ears. The eyesight and hearing of the Kees certainly owes a debt to the size and location of the organs designed for these purposes.

Eyes

The Keeshond has large, well-placed, widespread eyes that give it the visual capability to go along with its alertness. Not encumbered by heavy facial wrinkling or hair falling down over the eyes, the Keeshond is reminiscent of a fox or a wolf in its facial expression. Ever curious and watchful, the Keeshond seems to continually scan its surroundings. Keeshonden eyes reflect a good deal of natural intelligence and understated self-confidence, without any fight-or-flight manifestations.

Ears

Like its eyes, the Kees' ears are unhindered. The well-proportioned ears of the Keeshond are described as foxlike. As with the Pomeranian, the closest relative of the Keeshond, hearing is excellent.

Keeshond owners have many accounts of exceptional hearing in their dogs. One owner was awakened by a bark from the dog and alerted to the coughing of the owner's sick child in another part of the house. The dog not only heard the

Understanding the Keeshond

small child's coughs, but seemed insistent that something be done about it!

As with eyesight, the hearing ability of the Keeshond came not as a result of dog breeders' attempts to produce a better hunting or guard dog. The Kees naturally evolved over generations from dogs that lived with and listened for their humans.

Sense of Smell

The Keeshond has never been primarily thought of as a hunter. While some Keeshonden undoubtedly helped chase down vermin that preyed on the Dutch farms, the dog was never bred to specifically hunt anything. Still, the Keeshond's sense of smell is quite good. Some Kees have even become good ratters and rabbit dogs.

One breeder and exhibitor of Keeshonden told of a show champion male that led her to a fuse box where a burned-out circuit breaker had left a faint acrid odor. Another Kees person had a dog that detected the presence of a small child asleep in a hammock on the porch. While the owner and the Keeshond had been out for a walk, the child had wandered onto the porch, climbed into the hammock, and fallen asleep. The child's frantic parents were about to call the police when the Kees returned home, went immediately to where the child was sleeping, and barked a greeting.

Sense of Touch

Because the Keeshond is bred primarily for its companionability, it has a strong need for petting and physical contact with its owners. A Kees will often find a way to sit as close as possible to its human. Most Keeshonden require a daily ration of physical approval and affection from their human companions.

While definitely no softy, the Keeshond can be quite sensitive to neglectful or careless treatment. More than one Kees owner has seen a thoughtless or even unintended swat or blow cause the dog to sulk sadly until the misdeed by the human can be

made up or forgiven. Physical punishment is not recommended for any dog, but certainly not for a Keeshond. While the breed can take a great deal of physical hardship, physical punishment for a Keeshond hurts all the more because it comes from the human that the dog adores. The Kees doesn't need or deserve rough treatment.

American Kennel Club Standard for the Keeshond
General Appearance

The Keeshond (pronounced kayz-hawnd) is a natural, handsome dog of well-balanced, short-coupled body, attracting attention not only by its coloration, alert carriage, and intelligent expression, but also by its stand-off coat, its richly plumed tail well curled over its back, its foxlike expression, and its small pointed ears. Its coat is very thick around the neck and forepart of the

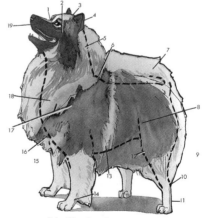

The anatomy of the Keeshond:

1. Stop	9. Hindquarters	17. Shoulder
2. Cheek	10. Hock	18. Brisket
3. Skull	11. Rear pastern	19. Muzzle
4. Ears	12. Stifle	
5. Neck	13. Rib cage	
6. Withers	14. Front pastern	
7. Tail	15. Forequarters	
8. Loin	16. Chest	

Understanding the Keeshond

The Keeshond's musculature reveals a sturdy, compact dog beneath that showy mass of coat.

shoulders and chest, forming a lionlike ruff (more profuse in the male). Its rump and hind legs, down to the hocks, are also thickly coated, forming the characteristic "trousers." Its head, ears, and lower legs are covered with thick, short hair.

The skeleton of a Keeshond shows the foundation of a squarely-made, well-balanced, short-coupled dog of medium size.

Size, Proportion, Substance

The Keeshond is a medium-size, square-appearing, sturdy dog, neither coarse nor lightly made. The ideal height of fully matured dogs when measured from top of withers to the ground is 18 inches (46 cm) for males and 17 inches (43.5 cm) for bitches (a one-inch [2.5 cm] variance either way is acceptable). While correct size is very important, it should not outweigh type.

Head

Expression: Expression depends largely on the distinctive characteristic called "spectacles"—a combination of markings and shadings in the orbital area that must include a delicate, dark line slanting from the outer corner of each eye toward the lower corner of each ear, coupled with expressive eyebrows. Markings (or shadings) on face and head must present a pleasing appearance, imparting to the dog an alert and intelligent expression. *Very serious fault:* Absence of dark lines that form the "spectacles."

Eyes: Eyes should be dark brown in color, of medium size, almond-shaped, set obliquely and neither too wide nor too close together. Eye rims are black. *Faults:* Round and/or protruding eyes or eyes light in color.

Ears: Ears should be small, triangular in shape, mounted high on head and carried erect. Size should be proportionate to the headlength, approximating the distance from the outer corner of the eye to the nearest edge of the ear. *Fault:* Ears not carried erect when at attention.

Skull: The head should be well-proportioned to the body and wedge-shaped when viewed from above. Not only the muzzle but the whole head should give this impression when the ears are drawn back by covering the nape of the neck and the ears with one hand. Head in profile should exhibit a definite stop. *Faults:* Apple head or absence of stop.

Muzzle: Of medium length, neither coarse nor snipey, and well-proportioned to the skull.

Understanding the Keeshond

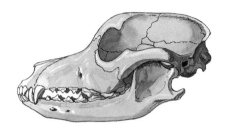

The skull of a Keeshond showing a definite stop. Viewed from the top, a Kees head should be wedge-shaped and in proportion to the dog's body.

Mouth: The mouth should be neither overshot nor undershot. Lips should be back and closely meeting — not thick, coarse or sagging — and with no wrinkle at the corner of the mouth. *Faults:* Overshot, undershot, or wry mouth.

Teeth: The teeth should be white, sound, and strong, meeting in a scissors bite. *Fault:* Misaligned teeth.

Neck, Topline, Body: The neck should be moderately long, well-shaped and well-set on the shoulders. The body should be compact with a short, straight back sloping slightly downward toward the hindquarters: well-ribbed, barrel well-rounded, short in loin, belly moderately tucked up, deep and strong of chest.

Tail: The tail should be moderately long and well-feathered, set on high and tightly curled over the back. It should lie flat and close to the body. The tail must form a part of the silhouette of the dog's body, rather than give the appearance of an appendage. *Fault:* Tail not lying close the back.

Forequarters: Forelegs should be straight seen from any angle. Pasterns are strong with a slight slope. Legs must be of good bone in proportion to the overall dog. Shoulder to upper arm angulation is between slight to moderate.

Hindquarters: Angulation in rear should be between slight to moderate to complement the forequarters, creating balance and typical gait.

Hindquarters are well-muscled, with hocks perpendicular to the ground.

Feet: The feet should be compact, well-rounded, catlike. Toes are nicely arched, with black nails.

Coat

The body should be abundantly covered with long, straight, harsh hair standing well out from a thick, downy undercoat. Head, including muzzle, skull, and ears, should be covered with smooth, soft, short hair — velvety in texture on the ears. The neck is covered with a mane — more profuse in the male — sweeping from under the jaw and covering the whole front part of the shoulders and chest, as well as the top part of the shoulders. The hair on the legs should be smooth and short, except for feathering down to the hocks — not below. The hair on the tail should form a rich plume. Coat must not part down the back. The

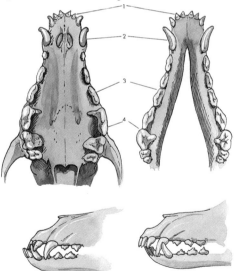

Keeshond Teeth:
Top Left — Upper Jaw: 1. incisors 2. canines 3. premolars 4. molars
Top Right — Lower Jaw: 1. incisors 2. canines 3. premolars 4. molars

Keeshond is to be shown in natural state, with trimming permitted only on feet, pasterns, hocks, and—if desired—whiskers. Trimming other than as described to be severely penalized. *Faults:* Silky, wavy, or curly coats. Part in coat down the back.

Color and Markings

A dramatically marked dog, the Keeshond is a mixture of gray, black, and cream. This coloration may vary from light to dark. The hair of the outer coat is black-tipped, the length of the black tips producing the characteristic shading of color. Puppies are often less intensely marked. The undercoat is very pale gray or cream, never tawny.

Head: The muzzle should be dark in color. "Spectacles" and shadings, as previously described, are characteristic of the breed and must be present to some degree. Ears should be very dark—almost black.

Ruff, Shoulders, and "Trousers": The color of the ruff and "trousers" is lighter than that of the body. The shoulder line markings of light gray must be well-defined.

Legs and Feet: Legs and feet are cream. *Fault:* Pronounced white marking. Black markings more than halfway down the foreleg, penciling excepted. White foot or feet.

Very Serious Faults

Entirely black or white or any solid color; any pronounced deviation from the color as described.

Gait

The distinctive gait of the Keeshond is unique to the breed. Dogs should move boldly and keep tails curled over the back. They should move cleanly and briskly; the movement should be straight and sharp, with reach and drive between slight to moderate.

Temperament

Temperament is of primary importance. The Keeshond is neither timid nor aggressive; rather, it is outgoing and friendly with both people and other dogs. The Keeshond is a lively, intelligent, alert, and affectionate companion.

The Keeshond Breeders Code of Ethics

One of the most progressive (and aggressive) breed club innovations to be enacted was the Keeshond Club Of America Code of Ethics, adopted in 1962. This code must be adhered to by all who wish to become members of this forward-thinking organization.

In brief, the code spells out standards of behavior for those who would breed Keeshonden. Only the healthiest, inherently sound, best temperament stock is to be used for breeding.

A Kees breeder following the Code has a placement plan for every puppy produced in the breeding program and sells healthy puppies to individuals and families, who receive all needed documentation (shot records, pedigrees, written directions on puppy care, and so forth).

The Code also stresses sanitary kennel conditions, rules regarding the allowable age of the bitches for breeding, and rules about studs being used only by other breeders who adhere to the tenets of the Code. The Code of Ethics even stipulates keeping prices at a reasonable level for quality dogs.

The Code is a blueprint for how all breeders should conduct themselves. Perhaps the most telling part of the Code is its adherence to a simple rule: in the absence of rules, how would I like to be treated myself? For a copy of this Code write to the Keeshond Club Of America (see Useful Addresses and Literature, page 77).

Before Buying A Keeshond

Before you buy a Keeshond, there are a number of questions to be answered. Failure to address these questions and honestly answer them could result in a mistake for which you, your family, or an innocent Keeshond could be penalized for years. Take time now to avoid possible heartache or regrets later.

Is the Keeshond Right for You?

By looking squarely at the pluses and minuses of the Keeshonden—as these relate to your personal lifestyle—you will be better able to make the right decision.

The beautiful, heavy coat of the Kees can be one of the breed's most attractive physical features or one if its specific negatives. Consider that dogs with such coats can shed quite a bit at times and will need regular (preferably daily) brushing and periodic grooming to look their best. Add to this potential "hairy" issue the fact that Kees really need and deserve to live with you in your home and you may have a serious concern to resolve. Are you, and each member of your household, able to accept into your house or apartment a dog that will occasionally leave hair around? (The Kees is no more a shedder than most other longhaired breeds, but you should deal with this question early in your considerations).

You already know about the Kees and its strong desire to be as close to you as possible. A second consideration for you is simply: Do you want to share your living arrangements with a dog? Do you have a lifestyle that will allow a dog to be included in most of the things you do?

Keeshonden breeders, groomers, veterinarians, and other people who work closely with dogs can attest to the intelligence of Keeshonden. While having a really smart dog can be a joy, it can also bring added responsibilities. A well-known Kees breeder and judge once referred to Keeshonden as "little, furry, three-year-old children." Perhaps her view exaggerates the smart-

The fun-loving, affectionate Keeshond has been aptly called the "Laughing Dutchman." (Notice the lighter colored areas circling the eyes—a charming breed characteristic called "spectacles.")

ness of the the breed a bit, but your consideration still remains, "Am I willing to do those needed extra things to help a bright dog become the best possible pet?"

Another consideration you must understand is the Keeshond's visual attractiveness, especially as a young puppy. A cute puppy, even a cute Keeshond puppy, is not some windup adorable toy that will run down and can be put on the shelf until it is convenient to bring it out again for play. Keeshonden breeders sometimes lament the fact that Kees pups have such appeal. Many a cute puppy can be purchased on a whim, and when the cuteness wears off it can be exiled first to some back room, then to the backyard, and finally to the dog pound. No puppy, Keeshond or not, deserves such inconsiderate and cruel treatment. A Keeshond will not be a passive member of your household. This bright, companionable dog will want to be a part of your family and a part of your life. Be doubly sure you have and want room in your life for an intelligent, impressionable canine.

Before Buying A Keeshond

Are You Right for the Keeshond?

To make this personal review you must be totally honest with yourself and your family. Set aside mental pictures about you and your devoted Kees strolling elegantly along the avenue or bedazzling friends with your dog's clever tricks. Someday you and your Keeshond may stroll and possibly even bedazzle, but much must be done before this vision can become reality!

Essential in your self-assessment is the fact that your Keeshond will look to you and your family for every aspect of its existence. Not only will you be supplying the obvious needs of water, food, shelter, and health care, but other not quite so obvious needs. You will be the socializing force in your Keeshond's upbringing, especially if that Keeshond comes to you as a puppy. You will be the guide to help your dog learn essential appropriate behaviors to be a good pet and a good canine citizen. You and your family will be the dog's main companions. As stated earlier, Keeshonden cannot endure the suburban equivalent of "junkyard dog" treatment—simply being left in the backyard with food and water. Kees need and thrive on human interaction, and if your living arrangements or schedules can't allow such close companionship, choose another breed of dog or perhaps don't choose a dog at all.

Assuming ownership of a Keeshond will mean assuming responsibility for the dog as a member of your family for perhaps 12 or 15 years. Kees ownership should not be initiated on an impulse or taken lightly. Before you and your family go much further down this path, answer these questions:

- Does each family member fully understand what is involved in Keeshond ownership?
- Has each person agreed to accept the work and responsibility a Kees will bring?
- Does each family member agree to give the Keeshond daily affection and attention?
- Can your family afford a new member who will require special food, grooming, and veterinary care?
- Is each person in your family willing to take time to help the Keeshond reach its potential as a good companion and family member?
- Does any family member suffer from allergies or conditions that a long-haired dog might aggravate?
- Will your family be willing to share space in your home with the Keeshond, not just as a cute puppy, but throughout its life?
- Has one specific, responsible family member agreed to be the primary care giver if your Kees is a young puppy?

These questions may seem obvious, but rest assured that neglecting to consider these areas can have inconvenient consequences for you and even tragic consequences for an innocent Keeshond. If you and your family have candidly answered these questions, you now have choices to ponder before you actually go Kees-searching.

The Kees is a sturdy, made-for-fun clown that will enjoy playing with its people, especially in the safety of a secured fenced yard!

18

Before Buying A Keeshond

Choice Number One—
A Puppy or an Older Dog

Your decision here can best be made by considering what you want in a Keeshond. If you want a show dog or an obedience ring dog, you would probably do well to choose a pup from exhibition and/or obedience breeding stock. If you are seeking a Kees for companion purposes, a puppy or an adult may suit your needs. Remember that a puppy will grow up with you and will be largely what you make it. An adult Kees may also be available, but you may need help from Keeshond breeders in your area or from the breed club itself to find an older pet that could fit into your life and home.

A puppy is much like a human baby. This cute little creature will need your love, attention, and care. Kees babies, while much faster maturing than human babies, will still feel fear in the middle of the night, make messes for you to clean, and require a lot of your time and attention.

Consistency is the key word in puppy care. You and your family will have to make the puppy's needs a priority. You can't be "too busy," "too tired," or "too anything" to care for a puppy. The benefits of Kees ownership are numerous, and the rewards of successfully bringing a fuzzy ball of Keeshond puppy into elegant, well-behaved adulthood are substantial, but these benefits and rewards don't come easy. They must be earned!

If you decide to bring an older Keeshond into your home, you can bypass much of the basic initial care a puppy will need. Even an older dog will need consistent attention, especially to readjust to a new family. Because Keeshonden form such strong bonds with their humans, some older dogs go through significant trauma when they are relocated. Fortunately, the intelligence of the breed and perhaps their spitz adaptability seem to help many adult dogs make a reasonably successful transition.

Of course there are dogs who may have learned bad habits or just different habits at their first home. Some of these dogs can be stubborn (which Kees breeders admit can be a trait of the breed). With the help of knowledgeable Kees people, you will probably be able to avoid those recalcitrant adults and find a dog that will do just fine. **Note:** Either way you go, puppy or adult, the use of the Keeshond breed club or respected breeders in your area will always be a wise move for you.

Choice Number Two—
A Male or a Female

As a breed, Keeshonden of either sex can make great pets. Both males and females can do well within the show ring or in obedience trials. Female Kees usually adapt well to family life and have a marked sweetness of disposition. They are slightly smaller on average than male Kees and are usually clearly feminine in appearance. Owners of female Keeshonden are enthusiastic about the devotion they show to their humans.

Male Kees are masculine without being excessively "macho." They have all the "strut" that one sees in most male dogs, but they aren't overly aggressive. As a pet, a male Kees would be able to be an equally good companion for rough-and-tumble children or for more sedate retirees.

As with most breeds, male and female Keeshonden each brings their own set of concerns to the dog owner. Males, for example, have the territorial habit of "marking" their property lines by urinating at certain points within their areas. This behavior in a housebroken dog will usually show itself only outside in the yard or when out on a walk.

Unspayed female Kees will go into heat during the estrus cycle about twice a year. During these times, they must be isolated from all non-neutered male dogs to prevent accidental breeding. Estrus-related discharge can also stain furniture or rugs and protective pads should be used to prevent this problem.

Your ultimate goals for your Keeshond must be taken into account here. If you have chosen not to pursue a career in the show ring for your female Kees, then certainly have her spayed (surgically rendered unable to go into estrus or produce puppies). Your spayed Keeshond will be just as sweet a companion as before, but she will not be "in season" twice yearly.

While a spayed female cannot be a show dog (American Kennel Club rules prohibit this) she certainly can compete in obedience trials. Spaying your pet quality dog (of any breed or mixture of breeds) is wise and responsible. You in no way affect the quality of the dog's companion abilities and you can, for all time, avoid those accidental matings that will produce more unwanted puppies in an already canine-cluttered world.

Your male Keeshond can be neutered (surgically altered). While he will keep all the vim and vitality of a male of his breed, your dog will not be as aggressive toward other males when in-season females are around. A neutered male will still retain all of his abilities to be an early-warning watchdog.

Unless you have, after long and serious thinking, decided you may want to try dog breeding, you should have your pet dogs either spayed or neutered.

Choice Number Three— Pet Quality or Show Quality

An acknowledged dog breeder once observed, "Really good show dogs come in groups—of one—and sometimes not even then!" Before you decide on a Kees puppy from either level—pet quality or show quality—an understanding of the terminology is necessary.

Trying to pick a potential champion Keeshond from a litter of woolly, squirming eight-week-old puppies is like trying to pick out a future senator or president by looking at human babies in a nursery. Therefore the designation "show quality" is merely a guess at best. This guess is based on the show qualities of a pup's parentage, plus years of experience with what other puppies looked like before they matured into show winners. Show puppy selection is, to say the least, an imprecise art.

Two show winners might produce a litter in which most or all the pups do not become show specimens. These nonwinners, if of good temperament and health, could be "pet quality" pups. Pet quality must always be considered in terms of health, temperament, and freedom from serious deformity. A pet puppy might have some minor defect in conformation or color, for example, that would eliminate it from the show ring. Such a puppy might, however, possess all the charm, devotion, and intelligence to make it just the canine companion for you and your family.

On the other hand, there may be a "show quality" puppy out there that would also be a superb pet. While potential show specimens may cost you a bit more at the outset, such a puppy may also be the right one for your household. Keeshonden, ever versatile, are quite capable of filling the bill as a pet, as a show dog, and as an obedience title holder. Even if you are looking only for a pet, you won't hurt yourself by starting with a top-notch show kennel. If a show-potential puppy is your choice, study the breed carefully. Attend as many dog shows as possible. Talk with a lot of Kees breeders. Try to find the breeder who seems to have the best all-round dogs, in show quality, health, intelligence, and temperament. Seek the best and you will come closer to finding what you want than by settling for the run-of-the mill, the average, the available.

Selecting a Keeshond Puppy

The more you know, the easier your search will be. Contact the Breed Club (see page 77) to

Before Buying A Keeshond

find out about Keeshond breeders and shows in your area. The Keeshond club and the breeders in your area can be a valuable resource in your quest for just that certain Kees that will be a member of your family for the coming decade or so.

Know what you want: young/old, male/female, show/pet quality. Listen to Keeshond people, who have pledged themselves to live up to the breeder's code of ethics (see page 16). Become familiar with these breeders and their dogs. Observe how show quality Kees are groomed for the show ring. Ask questions—even obvious questions. Most Kees people will be helpful to the novice who sincerely wants to learn.

Don't expect dedicated dog breeders (of any breed) to sell a top show prospect to a first-time dog owner. Dog breeders usually want such a puppy in the hands of an owner who will spend the time, money, and effort to give this pup the best possible exposure as a show dog.

Sometimes breeders may let a serious newcomer own a promising puppy in a partnership. In this way the breeder can help a neophyte dog fancier gain experience while assuring a candidate a favorable prospect of reaching its show ring potential.

Other breeders may help a potential show family obtain a good puppy that is uncertain as a show-winning prospect. In either case it will be up to you to win over the Keeshond breeders. Unless you can demonstrate that you can and will provide a good home for a Kees (either pet quality or show quality), don't expect them to help you get a puppy.

Finding a pet quality Kees will be somewhat easier (and somewhat cheaper), but expect reputable Keeshond breeders to still want to ensure that you will give a Kees puppy the best possible home. Many breeders will want to place a pet level puppy only on the proviso that this puppy will be spayed (if a female) or neutered (if a male). This is a common practice to prevent a lesser quality dog (by show standards) from being allowed to reproduce. Breeders will often with-hold a pup's registration papers until you provide documentation from a veterinarian that the dog has been spayed or neutered.

In buying a dog, remember the old dictum, "Buyer beware." For every responsible dog breeder who will help you find a good puppy there are several others to whom only your money is a motivation. Another old saying, "You get what you pay for" is equally applicable. Constantly keep in mind that you are not seeking to purchase an inanimate object. Your Kees choice will be a living, breathing, interacting member of your family for years to come. Don't make this important choice haphazardly or on an impulse.

You may be able to purchase or find a lead on a good Keeshond pup through your local pet store. You will certainly want to develop a friendship with a reputable pet store owner. Such a store might not only help you in finding a good quality puppy but will also be a ready source for food and other needed items for that puppy. A responsible pet store owner, who will want you to have the best possible outcome with a puppy, will be an important ally for you and your dog.

Again, know exactly what you are seeking prior to the search. If you want a show prospect, seek such a pup from an acknowledged show Keeshond source. If you are attracted to obedience training and obedience trials with your Kees, search for a dog from parentage that has shown success in this area.

If at all possible, you should try to see the father and mother of your prospective puppy. Remember that a mother Kees may not look her best after birthing and raising a healthy litter. You can, however, look at her overall health, temperament, and general breed characteristics. (Put less emphasis on her coat, which may have suffered somewhat from her maternity.)

Regardless of your secondary goals for your Keeshond (show, obedience) keep in mind that you are primarily seeking a friend and companion dog. You should want a healthy puppy with a sound temperament that will join your family and become an important and successful part of it. Since such a canine family member is what you really want (and it certainly should be), if you settle for anything else you will regret it, probably for years.

After you have assessed your own (and your family's) readiness for Keeshond ownership, and have decided what you really desire in a Kees, you are almost ready for the actual selection process. Before you choose a pup from any source, you must be certain that the following are available:

- The puppy's complete medication and worming records with dates.
- A health certificate, signed by the breeder's veterinarian attesting that the puppy has been examined and found healthy.
- The American Kennel Club (AKC) Registration certificate, which confirms that your Keeshond is purebred. (You should also receive an application that, when sent to the AKC, will let you register your puppy in your own name. A spay/neuter agreement for a pet quality pup may affect immediate receipt of this form.)
- Your Kees' pedigree showing its parents, grandparents, and other lineage. (Remember that a pedigree is only as good as the source you have chosen for your puppy. If you don't feel this source is absolutely trustworthy, you probably won't feel much better about the pedigree.)

This documentation is important. If it is not available, forget about buying a puppy there. Reputable Kees sources will supply all these documents as a matter of course. Many reputable dog breeders will also insist that *you* provide some documentation in addition to a possible spay/neuter agreement. Responsible breeders accept the puppies they allow to be born as lifetime responsibilities and may expect the following things from you, before they will sell you a puppy:

- A return agreement specifying that should things change in your life or if it should happen

that you just can't keep the Keeshond, that it will be returned to the breeder rather than being disposed of in another manner (sold, given away, euthanized, or sent to the pound).
- A statement that you understand the special needs of a Keeshond and agree to provide for these needs in an acceptable manner.

If all the paperwork is available and you have confidence in this source (based on your homework about Keeshonden and about the various options available to you), selection time is at hand!

Keeshond pups are adorable. A litter of healthy, active puppies is a delight to observe. In some ways you are now embarked on the most difficult part of your selection process. Herein lies the reason for all your prior planning. If a male show prospect puppy is what you are seeking, ask the breeder or owner to isolate all the male pups with exhibition potential. By narrowing your selection to what you have decided you want, you won't have to resist the cute females or any obvious pet pups as you make your choice.

Carefully observe each puppy candidate, since show prospects are never plentiful. You must keep in mind that a six-to-eight week-old puppy will not show its full potential. You also know that these puppies may have had limited contact with people other than their breeders. Such puppies may show some initial apprehension when confronted by strangers. Kees puppies are generally a gregarious and friendly lot and will usually get over any early misgivings about you. Be patient and calm. Watch the puppies watching you. It is, of course, important to involve your family in every step of this process.

You may immediately find the ideal puppy. If you don't, don't weaken now. You have carefully and realistically planned for just the right age, sex, and quality level that you want. Unless you are willing to throw all your efforts out the window and pick the first cute pup you see, you must stick to your plan. **Note:** If you are seeking only a companion and pet and the gender and show potential are unimportant, then you possibly could pick the first pup you see. Even so, you would be better off seeing several litters, even if you eventually go back and select that first puppy anyway.

Kees puppies are not usually a glut on the market. Most responsible breeders plan only a few litters each year. If you have made friends with a reputable Keeshond breeder, you might put your name on a waiting list for a puppy from an upcoming litter. Some breeders require a deposit to hold a puppy for you in this manner. Under any arrangement, don't become fixated and settle on a particular puppy as your final choice until *your* veterinarian has had a chance to examine it. Extra effort now can help you avoid possible heartache later.

Choosing a Keeshond puppy may seem to be a protracted activity, but you are choosing a puppy who could be around for many years. When you think of this puppy as a family member, you can see the importance of making such a choice with as much care as possible. Take time now to do everything you can to ensure that your coming Keeshond years are great ones!

Picking Up a Puppy Safely and Correctly

Though Kees pups are not especially fragile, you and your family should know the right way to handle this friendly, fuzzy, squirming bit of young canine. Always move slowly and gently; support the back and rear end with one hand and the chest with another. In this manner the puppy will feel more secure as you look it over. **Note:** If you are visiting more than one Keeshond litter at different homes in the same day, act responsibly by washing your hands (or perhaps cleansing them with one of those handy antibacterial wipes). You certainly would not want to be responsible for carrying any illness from one litter to another.

Always use care when picking up a puppy. Remember to support both its rear and hind legs with one hand while steadying its chest with the other. Each member of your family should know how to pick up and hold a puppy safely.

Keeshonden and Children

Kees and kids sometimes seem to have been invented for each other. As a sturdy spitz breed, the Keeshond is able to take a good deal of active play and roughhousing with children. It is wise, however, to supervise very small children constantly as they play with a dog, and most certainly with a puppy.

One adult Keeshond found a way to control things when playing with unintentionally rough children. In its human family were robust twin boys. These twin toddlers were allowed to play in a large playpen in the family front yard; often the Kees female would jump into the playpen. When the twins' play got too rough, she would simply jump out again and watch over the active little boys from outside, from just beyond hair-pulling range!

Before Buying A Keeshond

Children and Keeshonden get along well together, but it is always advisable to supervise very young children when they play with any pet.

The safety of the dog should always be a major concern. Common sense will tell you that a very young child could unintentionally hurt a very young puppy. In a few months or a year, the same child would know more about how to act around a pet and the pet better able to withstand the rough play and tight hugs of some children. Children and Keeshonden get along well together if the children are taught to be kindly and responsible.

Keeshonden and the Family

As mentioned, the Kees is a good dog for the family group. Some breeds will become attached to one member and more or less just tolerate the other people in the home. Keeshonden don't usually show this behavior. Thriving as they do on affection and human interaction, most Kees really enjoy "owning" several humans.

One Keeshond female seemed to attach itself to different family members at different times of the day. In the morning she helped the mother get the family off for the day. After school she stayed close to the children, playing with them in the yard. At night, she contented herself with remaining near the father's chair and watching television.

Keeshonden and Older People

Many older people have found in the Kees a pet/companion that fits well with what can be a somewhat restrained lifestyle. Keeshonden are, if properly raised and trained, quite content to be close to their human companions on either an active or sedentary schedule.

Some older people have asserted that daily brushing of a Keeshond, combined with regular walks, not only met the dog's needs, but established a good exercise regimen. The Kees' adaptability and loving nature make it a good choice for a person at any age.

Christmas and Gift Puppies

Contrary to an almost traditional vision about puppies as Christmas gifts, this is *not* a good idea. Bringing a bewildered puppy into the happy chaos that is Christmas morning is neither smart nor kind. A puppy will need a lot of care and attention. The timing is all wrong for the puppy to get what it needs when the family is absorbed with other gifts, holiday festivities, and activities. In the best of situations the chance for neglect exists when so many other things draw attention away from the new puppy. A few weeks before Christmas or a few weeks after Christmas would be fine—just not on Christmas day.

One well-known Keeshond breeder tells those who inquire about Christmas puppies that she will sell them a puppy at Christmas provided the puppy is the *only* gift exchanged in the family that Christmas. This seems to get the point across.

Before Buying A Keeshond

Another dog breeder devised a creative and caring way to "give a puppy for Christmas." This breeder makes available, as part of the price for an after-Christmas puppy, a short video on the breed, on puppy care, and what owning a puppy will mean. Added to this standard video is a message specifically directed to the child or children of the household. As the breeder holds a cute puppy, she speaks to each child by name and alerts them that in a few weeks a puppy like this one is coming to live at their house. She encourages the children to learn what the puppy will need and to help their parents prepare for it. (Such a video might also be a good alternative gift for that kindly uncle or grandparent, or even for that impulsive mom or dad who wants to surprise a child on its birthday with a puppy.)

Keeshonden and Other Animals

The Kees can certainly learn to adjust to other pets in its home, but some Keeshonden do like to be the main pet. Thoughtful humans will understand that a dog bred primarily to be a companion may not like sharing its humans with other animals. Some dogs will require more help here than others, and beginning early to help a pup adjust to other animals in the home certainly is advisable.

Cats normally don't have much to fear from Keeshonden. Some owners tell of good, lifelong friendships between the family cat and the family Kees. This is often also the case with other dogs in the family. In any event, good owner judgment and common sense can prevent most animal altercations.

Not pugnacious by nature, the Kees exudes a sense of happy confidence that usually keeps it out of trouble during encounters with unfamiliar dogs. However, the Keeshond is also not cowardly and will hold its ground during confrontations. Possessing a heavy coat that it may bristle impressively to warn off a would-be attacker, the Keeshond generally would rather peacefully coexist. If trouble isn't wise enough to stay away, the physically sturdy Kees can, if necessary, back up its bristle with muscle.

Caring For Your Keeshond

Before You Bring Your Keeshond Home

Bringing a new puppy, or even an adult dog, into your home to become an integral part of your family can be quite an experience—for you and for the dog. Take reasonable care to make the homecoming as enjoyable and untraumatic as possible—for both of you.

Perhaps while you are still searching for that special Kees, you could take some preparatory steps to assure your new pet the best possible environment:

• With the breeder's permission, you could plan a trip with your family to see how an experienced Kees person lives with one or more dogs at home. Such a visit could give you invaluable pointers on the ways a serious breeder lives and interacts with members of the breed you are considering—the Keeshond.

• Most breeders, after they realize your sincerity as a potential Keeshond owner, will be pleased to give you ideas on how to Kees-proof your home. You could possibly invite such a breeder to visit your household before you purchase a puppy and get advice. One Keeshond fancier owned a very affable dog that had been rescued from the dog pound. This Kees person would "loan" out this friendly dog to select prospective families that had never owned a Keeshond before. These visits, usually for a weekend or even for just a few hours, gave potential owners a chance to see how a Keeshond could fit into their home environment. Of course, not every breeder is willing to give you a "trial spin" with a dog, but most might agree to drop by with a dog for you to see within the confines of your own home.

While adult dogs will experience some transition trauma upon a move to a new home, it is usually the puppies that will need the most preparation and attention. Puppies are making a double adjustment. Not only have they been taken away

Tatooing your pet for easy identification is a good safeguard that really does not cause the dog very much discomfort. Discuss this with your veterinarian.

from the familiar surrounding of mother and litter mates, but they are undergoing mental and physical changes at a very rapid rate. Helping a puppy make these early adjustments is not only necessary to help ensure a good future canine companion, but is basic kindness.

Some Things You Will Need

Some purchases will be necessary to outfit your new Keeshond. One of the most important will be a dog cage, carrier (airline-type), or crate. (See the chapter, Training Your Keeshond, page 54.) A cage/crate/carrier will be very helpful in providing a den or "lair" for your Kees. All dogs, Keeshonden included, are denning animals. As such, they need to have a special place that is

A Kees mother dog will usually provide her pups with the basic lessons they need. Responsible owners will help the youngsters grow into their full pet potential.

For those times when your Keeshond has to be outside, a well-constructed dog house will provide protection from the weather.

uniquely theirs within the larger confines of their home with you. This lair or den will also be a very handy training aid when housebreaking your puppy.

You should purchase two sturdy, flat-bottomed bowls—one for water, one for food. These bowls should not be easily tipped over. It is also handy for food and water dishes to be dishwasher-safe and microwave-safe.

If at all possible, purchase some of the very same food the puppy has been eating. A new home is stressful enough on the newcomer. Don't add to the stress by changing diets. If the puppy's breeder has had success with a particular dog

Keeshonden puppies are among the most appealing of any breed, but they will only thrive if given lots of love, consistent care, a safe place to live, and adequate training.

food, stay with it. There is ample time for change after this crucial transition period of puppyhood has passed.

Your young Keeshond will need a good leash and collar. (See Training Equipment, page 60.) These should be the right size for an active puppy and of strong construction for use with a puppy not yet leash trained. Because you must maintain control of the puppy when it is outside, a leash and collar are important both for safety and early training.

Your reliance on an experienced Kees person is wise also in the initial purchase of grooming equipment. Get a high-quality grooming comb and brush. As you will soon see, setting the stage for a well-groomed adult Keeshond begins with making regular grooming a pleasant experience for both you and the young dog.

Keeshonden, like their little cousins, the Pomeranians, need toys, both to play with and to "own." The possession of such playthings by puppies and adults dogs alike sometimes takes on the same significance as a security blanket or favorite stuffed animal with a young child. Additionally, sturdy, well-made dog toys serve a function as a teether for chew-oriented young puppies. Your pet shop contact can help you find some good toys for your puppy.

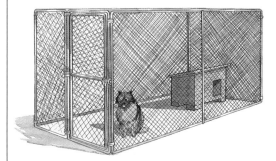

Most dog experts point out that the Keeshond should not be kept shut up outside in a kennel away from you and your family. If you don't want to share your home with your Kees, perhaps you should reconsider owning one.

"Puppy-proofing" Your Home

In addition to making all the necessary purchases *prior* to your puppy's arrival at your home, you must turn your attention to making your home safe for an inquisitive puppy.

"Puppy-proofing" your home for your new Keeshond is a two-phase operation. In phase one take a hard look at your home, especially those places where the puppy will live. Look for any possible danger area. Stairwells and narrow spaces behind large furniture or appliances where a curious puppy might get trapped are sites to block off or eliminate. Low-level vents in laundry rooms or bathrooms (where unsupervised puppies are often left) must have strong protective grids. Even seemingly harmless areas behind a door or near sinks, toilets, or bathroom drains could cause injury to an unaware young puppy. One Kees breeder related a story where a puppy left in a laundry room found and ate a small sliver of hand soap and became quite ill, causing the new owner a great deal of anguish. Another puppy, confined to a bathroom, licked up some drain cleaner that had been spilled and had gone unnoticed. Sadly, this puppy did not survive.

Try to think like an inquisitive puppy. Seek out places where even remotely possible danger might exist. Open fireplaces, heavy items that might fall on a small puppy, sharp points or edges can all cause injury to a young, impulsive puppy.

Phase two in puppy-proofing involves searching out all items that might prove injurious to a licking, chewing puppy. Tacks, pins, pesticides, lead-based painted woodwork or furniture, some house and yard plants can all be dangerous to a young puppy. As mentioned, household chemicals and cleaners can do great harm. Even the fumes from cleaning fluids used on rugs, drapes, or upholstery can sometimes cause illness to the puppy who comes in contact with them. Electrical wires can kill a chewing puppy as quickly as a speeding automobile.

Not just inside the home, but in the yard and on the driveway there are hazards. One of the greatest dangers to dogs of all ages is the ingestion of antifreeze, which can leak from a car's radiator onto a street, sidewalk, or driveway. Added to the very poisonous nature of antifreeze is the fact that dogs seem to love the taste of it.

A new puppy in the home always brings added responsibilities. While it is strongly suggested that one responsible person in your household be given the primary role of taking care of the new Kees puppy, every family member should also play a part. This is especially true with regard to keeping the puppy safe from harm.

Bringing Your Puppy Home

After you are certain about your Kees-puppy-proofed home, you should coordinate with the puppy source to bring your puppy home at the best possible time.

Your puppy will be leaving a world it knows, perhaps leaving its mother and litter mates. Several days of adjustment will be very important. You or someone else will need to have several days at home to assist the puppy in becoming comfortable in its new home. As stated, bringing a puppy home is not unlike bringing home a new baby. Some breeders make a point of insisting that new puppy owners take several days of vacation (if necessary) to just be around the home to help the new pup settle in. Extra efforts taken at the beginning can pay off for years to come with a pet/companion that has become a well-adjusted member of your family.

A car trip may be no major event to you, but to an eight-week-old Kees puppy it can be frightening. Remember that your puppy may have never even seen an automobile before and now it has to get inside one in the company of strangers, and travel in the strange machine to who-knows-where.

Caring For Your Keeshond

While the cage/crate/carrier mentioned earlier will very shortly be of importance to you and your pup, it is advisable to let your new puppy ride to its new home in the secure, but gentle grasp of an adult or older child. If the puppy is already acquainted with this person, even better still. Be sure to have the designated "puppy holder" bring an old robe and some towels in case the puppy gets car sick.

After this first trip to its new home, your puppy will ideally feel quite comfortable riding with you in the family car. As befits a breed with a nickname like the "Dutch barge dog," Keeshonden usually enjoy traveling. Because traveling with your dog can add so much to pet ownership, make every effort to make this first trip a pleasant one.

If you must travel for several hours to bring your puppy home, be certain to build into your schedule frequent stops or "relief breaks." Your puppy's bladder will not have its full holding capacity yet. Be sure to walk the puppy at least once each hour of the trip to give it an opportunity for urination or defecation.

Older dog or puppy, don't allow your Keeshond to have free run of the car while it is moving. There are simply too many opportunities for injury from sudden stops, sharp turns, or steep inclines to risk letting the Kees wander around unrestrained.

Upon reaching your home, your puppy's training can begin even before it goes inside. Since you have probably set aside some area where you intend to walk your pet, start things off right. Take the newcomer immediately to this preselected area and allow it to nose around and explore. (Some experts suggest even bringing some used litter from the puppy's first home to "salt the mine" and encourage the puppy to defecate or urinate at this spot.) This is the first important step in housebreaking. Wait patiently with your puppy until it makes use of the special area, then heap on the praise. Let the puppy know that it has done just the right thing, in just the right spot, at just the right time.

This is your first big chance to reinforce positive behavior in the Keeshond that will be your pet and companion for years to come. From now on, but especially in the tender, formative period of puppyhood, you should use praise to signal the animal that it has your approval, acceptance, and love for doing what comes naturally at this particular place. If you start this practice very early and consistently continue it, housebreaking your smart, young Keeshond should be a snap. **Note:** *Never* punish or scold the dog at the relief spot. This will only send confusing, mixed messages to your pet. The only response from you at this location should be a positive one.

After your puppy's first successful urination/defecation session, you are ready to introduce your new canine family member to your already Kees puppy-proofed living quarters. Now is a good time to introduce the cage/crate/carrier that will fulfill the crucial requirement for a "den" for your Keeshond.

You may have borrowed an old blanket or towel from your pup's former home. You may have brought along one of your puppy's favored toys (perhaps even one that you introduced to it sometime before you were ready to bring the puppy home). You have placed these reminders of its mother and litter mates in the appropriately sized crate that you have obtained just for this special puppy. You have placed this crate in an out-of-the-way but not isolated place in your home. You are almost ready to introduce the puppy to its den.

When your Kees first comes into your home, you will want to let the pup get acquainted with its new humans and its new surroundings. Play gently with the puppy. (If it makes any sign to wet or mess on the floor, quickly pick it up and go out to the special spot for this purpose. When it uses the right location, use lots of praise.) When your puppy begins to get tired, as puppies will after a few minutes of playing, take the puppy and place it in its den. Shut the door and walk away.

You want the puppy to associate "tired" with the den where it is to rest and sleep. With many

Kees puppies, this lesson is so easily learned after consistent repetition, that they will seek out the crate and go in when they are tired, all on their own initiative! This lesson is the most important, after housebreaking, that you can teach your puppy.

Your puppy will now have to learn about being away from the familiar surroundings of its mother and litter mates. While this is an adjustment for the puppy, it will also be an adjustment for you and your family! Your puppy must learn that when it is placed in the den/crate at night that it must go to sleep. You and your family must learn to let the puppy learn its lesson. An early rule for you and each member of your household is that nobody gives in to feeling sorry for the lonely, crying puppy in its crate. If someone slips in and takes the whimpering, crying puppy out of its crate and cuddles it, the puppy will learn a big lesson: "The best way I can get out of this crate is to whine, whimper, and cry enough and someone will come to let me out and hold me."

A crying, sad puppy is nobody's idea of a pleasant thing, but a crying, sad (and neurotic) adult dog is even worse. Your puppy will not die or even be harmed by being left in its crate alone at night. This is one of those adjustments that a pet dog must make on its way to becoming a good companion. Animal shelters and dog pounds are full of dogs that were not taught (or allowed to learn) this lesson.

There are, of course, ways to make the lonely vigil of your puppy a little easier. You can speak to the dog in a calm and reassuring voice, but don't overdo it. You just want to let the puppy in its den know that you are nearby. You have already put some familiar-smelling things in the crate. You might add an old fashioned, nonleaking, hot water bottle to simulate the warmth of its mother and brothers and sisters. (An electric heating pad is a bad idea for lots of reasons. Just don't do it). Some people have had success with an old ticking alarm clock (again nonelectric, please!) to serve as a replacement for the mother dog's heartbeat. A modern idea that has some following is to set a radio on an all-night talk station on low volume, just outside the den and out of the puppy's reach in the daytime.

Again, of all the factors to make your pup's first lonely nights successful, consistency ranks the highest. If you help the puppy by not giving in to its cries, the ordeal may last only a few days. If someone in the family does give in, the ordeal could last for years!

Preferably, you have already purchased some of the very same food that the puppy has been eating before you brought it home. If at all possible, this is no time for a diet change. Your puppy will be going through enough transitions; changing its food and possibly bringing on digestive problems or diarrhea is not a wise move at all. Your puppy may have some stress-related diarrhea anyway, but if it lasts only for a couple of days, it shouldn't be cause for alarm. If it continues longer call your veterinarian just to be on the safe side.

Your adventure with your new puppy has just begun. Properly handled, this can be one of the most gratifying experiences of your life. Handled improperly, it can be one of the most frustrating. Rest assured that the first days are usually the toughest as well as among the most important. Follow the advice of your dog's breeder, your veterinarian, or your friend at the pet supply shop on how to make things go easier. The time spent now will be amply repaid in a currency of great value — the devotion of a healthy and well-adjusted Keeshond as an integral part of your family probably for the next decade or longer.

Traveling with Your Keeshond

Adaptability is a byword of most of the spitz breeds. The Keeshond is no exception to this when it comes to traveling. The ancestors of today's Kees often lived on barges and boats, with new locales an everyday experience.

Caring For Your Keeshond

Your Keeshond can definitely be a part of your travel plans. While some individual dogs (in every breed) enjoy moving around more than others, most Kees should be flexible enough to let their owners take them on trips of varying lengths. Successful traveling with any pet, however, hinges on planning and preparation. By taking time to think through your trip and by taking a few simple steps to be ready, you help assure your pet's comfort and safety.

Traveling By Car

From short trips about town to extended motor vacations, many Kees owners regularly take their pets with them with excellent results. Traveling with your Keeshond by car need not be an overly bothersome activity, if you follow these basic rules of the road:

- When your car is in motion with your dog inside it, *always* have your Kees either in a carrier or securely fastened in a canine seat belt or safety harness.
- Absolutely *never* leave your dog in a parked car (even with the windows partially rolled down) during daylight hours when the outside temperature is as high as 60°F (16°C) (see Heatstroke, page 51).
- Even if your Kees is a robust, outdoor-type, don't let it ride in the back of an open pickup truck. While this might look like fun for the dog, there are about a thousand things that could happen to your dog, and all of them are bad!
- If you are thinking of traveling on a reasonably long trip with your Keeshond, check with your veterinarian before you go. Ask about feeding restrictions before and during the trip and about the advisability of motion sickness medications for your dog.
- On trips of several hours or more, be sure to have rest and relief breaks every hour. Give your dog some exercise and a drink of water too. *Always* keep even a well-behaved dog on a leash during these recesses.

- Plan ahead for hotel/motel accommodations. Most auto clubs, travel guides, and most large hotel/motel chains can tell you which inns allow pets in their guests' rooms. Don't assume that you will find lodging for you and your pet where ever you want to stop. Never try to slip your dog into a hotel or motel where pets are not allowed. This is rude and, in some cases, against the law!

Traveling By Air

Some years ago you were taking a chance when you tried to fly with your dog. Today airline travel is much safer, more comfortable, and more convenient for dog owners traveling with their pets. Most domestic and overseas airlines now welcome canine passengers.

If your dog's "den" is something other than an approved carrier, you can usually rent a carrier from the airline. An approved carrier and what could be called the "Ten Rules of Canine Air Travel" are important in making the skies a littler friendlier for you and your potentially airborne Keeshond.

1. Know the regulations and informal suggestions of any airline you are planning to use *before* you make reservations for you and your Keeshond.

2. Visit the veterinarian to inquire whether there are any reasons your Keeshond shouldn't travel by air at this time. Your veterinarian can also provide the health certificate that most airlines are now requiring for pet passengers (and which must be dated no more than ten days before the day you plan to fly). You can also ask about any medications (motion sickness medicine or tranquilizers) your dog's doctor thinks may be needed.

3. Make your flight reservations (and those of your dog) well before the day you plan to travel. If at all possible, try to get a direct flight, even if you have to drive to the nearest "hub" airport to do so. This will eliminate the need for a change of

flights that could cause your pet to be delayed or sent to a location different from yours.

4. Arrive early and insist on being allowed to see your dog and its carrier being loaded on the same flight you are to take. By handling this in advance you shouldn't run into too many obstacles.

5. If you are traveling to another country, be doubly sure to meet all entry requirements for coming in (and then being allowed to leave) with a pet. One Kees' owner and a regular foreign traveler always has duplicates of all documentation. One set is always on his person while traveling.

6. Whether you are using your Keeshond's own carrier or have rented one, carefully go over it to be sure that all the nuts and bolts are tight, the door and latch are in good working order, and that the "conversion kit" water dish can be filled from outside the carrier. Some dog owners attach a small padlock to secure the carrier door.

7. Be certain that "Live Animal" stickers are prominently placed on the carrier and that you have securely attached a luggage tag with your name, your home telephone number, and a telephone number where you can be reached at your destination.

8. A clean blanket or carrier pad along with a favorite toy will make the carrier more comfortable and a little less forbidding to your Keeshond (especially for a first-time flier).

9. Do not feed your pet for four to six hours before takeoff. Water can be given up to two hours before departure time. This would also be a good time for some exercise and a relief walk. Remember not to put food or water (other than in the conversion kit water dish) in the carrier. While you might put a favorite kind of rawhide chew, food will only make the carrier messy and uncomfortable for your Kees. **Note:** Unless you are absolutely certain that you can obtain your dog's specific brand of food at your destination, be sure to pack enough in *your* luggage to last the trip. Also

include any medicines that your dog may need during its journey.

10. In dealing with airline personnel, be firm, but polite. Make them realize the furry, silver dog peering out of the carrier is of great importance and value to you. Ask for (and write down) the names of the airline employees with whom you are entrusting your pet. One dog breeder always takes pictures of her dog being placed in the carrier and then of the carrier being turned over to the airline personnel.

Boarding Your Keeshond

There are situations where you cannot, or should not, take your dog with you on a trip. Very old dogs or puppies may not do well on an extended trip, for example. You may find that you have to consider alternatives, such as boarding your pet. Even here you have several options.

• You may have a friend, neighbor, or family member who can care for your pet, perhaps even in its own home.

• A whole, relatively new, industry has sprung up with pet sitters available to provide competent care for your pet, in its own home, while you are away. Always ask for references and then always check them before turning your home and dog over to this pet sitter.

• Your veterinarian or groomer may board your Kees and would already be familiar with and to your dog.

• Your Keeshond's breeder, if nearby, may be able to take back this old friend for a few days.

• There are many high-quality boarding kennels that are accredited by (and must live up to the strict standards of) the American Boarding Kennel Association (ABKA) (see Useful Addresses and Literature, page 77).

Feeding Your Keeshond

The Importance of a Balanced Diet

One of the great ironies of pet ownership centers around a pattern into which some people fall. They go out into the purebred dog marketplace. They seek out a dog of reasonably good quality, buy this dog and all the assorted paraphernalia that can go with it. They have a veterinarian give the dog a comprehensive checkup. Then, after all that time, effort, and expense, many people pay little or no attention to the food they feed this dog.

What and how you feed your Keeshond (or your beagle or your Bouvier des Flandres for that matter) will have a direct and ongoing effect on the physical and mental health of the dog. In fact, your dog's diet may even determine how long it will live.

Your Kees will, first and foremost, need a balanced diet. By "balanced" pet nutritionists mean a diet that is nutritionally complete — one that contains all the elements your Keeshond will need to grow and to build strong bones, teeth, hair, and muscle.

There are three primary rules to follow in feeding your Kees.
- Find a high quality nutritionally balanced dog food and feed it consistently.
- Don't feed your dog more than it needs, even if it wants more.
- Absolutely no table scraps!

Basic Nutrition

A balanced, nutritionally complete diet will contain what I call the "Seven Pillars of Good Canine Nutrition": proteins, carbohydrates, fats, vitamins, minerals, good drinking water, and owner knowledge and consistency.

Your pet won't be any better than the food you feed it. Find a quality food, stay on it and avoid table scraps!

Proteins

Proteins give your Kees the necessary amino acids essential for growth, development of strong muscles and bones, the ongoing maintenance of bones and muscles, and their repair in event of injury. Proteins also help in another way when a dog is sick or hurt; they promote the production of infection-battling antibodies. In addition, protein is important in the production of the enzymes and hormones needed for the everyday chemical processes that go on inside your Keeshond.

Good sources of protein in a dog food are meat, poultry, milk products, fish meal, and soybeans.

Carbohydrates

Carbohydrates are, along with fats, the "fuels" that put the "go" in your Kees. Measured in calories, carbohydrates in dog foods generally come from thoroughly cooked grains and vegetable ingredients. Processed starches also are some common sources of carbohydrates. High quality canine diets do not neglect the importance of carbohydrates. Some dog foods designed for older dogs emphasize carbohydrates over fats as a way to hold down undesired weight.

Fats

Fats are a much more concentrated energy source. Fats provide double the available energy as the same amount of carbohydrates. Fats also help transport the fat-soluble vitamins, A, D, E, and K. Among other important functions, these vitamins promote healthy hair and skin.

Fats also are significant in maintaining your Keeshond's nervous system. Fats, in addition to their vital roles in metabolism, also make foods taste better to dogs (as they do to humans). This is important if the dog is to relish its food, eat it readily, and take in the necessary amount for good nutrition.

Vitamins

One of the misunderstood areas in canine nutrition involves vitamins. A high quality, balanced dog food will provide your dog with all the vitamins it will normally need. In most cases, there is no need for dietary supplements.

Minerals

Minerals are musts for the regular health and normal body functioning of your dog. Calcium and phosphorus are necessary for the development and maintenance of strong bones, muscles, and teeth. Sodium and potassium aid in regulating body fluids and in nervous system maintenance. Iron promotes healthy blood in your Kees.

Mineral supplements should not be necessary. A good dog food, chosen with care, will provide all the minerals your dog will normally need or can assimilate. As with vitamins, consult with a canine nutritionist or veterinarian before adding minerals to a nutritionally balanced canine diet.

Water

One of the most important components of your Keeshond's diet comes right out of your water tap. Water, of course, works in concert with dog food to provide needed liquids for system functioning. Water also plays a role in respiration and in cooling a dog's system.

Water should be pure, fresh, and ample. Water bowls should be washed regulary with warm water and detergent, rinsed thoroughly, and kept full.

Studies have shown that water laden with bacteria or algae is not only unattractive to you, but possibly a danger to your dog. The quality and appearance of your dog's water should be as good as that of your drinking water.

Knowledge and Consistency

Protein, carbohydrates, fats, vitamins, minerals, and water are all key elements of a balanced and healthful diet for your dog. These components could be of little or no value to your dog without what you bring to a balanced diet—your knowledge and your consistency.

Your Keeshond will be totally dependent on you for its food. By taking time to understand what constitutes a good dog food over a not-so-good dog food, you will be better able to fulfill your responsibility.

After you have made certain that a particular food fits the needs of your Kees, be consistent with the food. Don't be swayed by cute ads, bargain deals, or fads. Your dog will function much better on the same quality food fed in the same way every day than on a hodge podge of different foods on an erratic schedule. Your dog's system needs time to adjust to a new food. Consistency is a crucial element in canine nutrition.

Feeding Your Keeshond

Commercial Dog Food

Pet foods are a multibillion dollar business in the United States. There is an ever-growing number of dog food brands making their way into the marketplace, and all of them are targeting your dog as a potential consumer. Your Keeshond (smart though it may be) will never buy dog food for itself, so yours is the task of learning about the available products.

There are a good number of excellent dog foods on the market. There are also an equal or greater number of foods that are less than the best. By doing a little homework you can discover which will be best for you and your dog.

Learn how to read dog food labels and identify dog food ingredients to know just what is in the food that goes into your Kees.

These labels, ingredient lists, and product analysis are required, by law, to be on containers of dog food. As with human foods, the ingredients listed are in descending order of their quantity in the formula. The first three or four ingredients can make up as much as 80 to 85 percent of the total dog food. This leaves only 15 to 20 percent to include any other feed product ingredients, all the minerals, vitamins, and other elements.

Percentages of protein, fat, fiber, and moisture are also specified on a dog food bag; protein, fat, and moisture percentages are printed on a can label. These are important to your feeding program for your Kees. Different levels of protein and/or fat, for example, are needed for different phases in a dog's life. When in doubt, talk to experienced Keeshond breeders, your veterinarian, and knowledgeable pet store personnel about the needs of your particular pup or dog. Also useful are the toll-free telephone numbers of many of the good dog food companies. Ask questions and expect answers that make sense to you.

Premium dog foods are more expensive than the mass appeal products that are in the marketplace. In buying dog food it is generally a good idea to remember that, like buying anything else, "you get what you pay for." In the long run, cheap, poor-quality foods can often be very expensive.

Premium foods are generally found in pet and pet supply stores, specialty feed stores, some veterinarians, some groomers, and some boarding kennels.

Commercial dog foods are generally manufactured in three formulations: canned, semimoist, and dry. Each has its advantages and disadvantages.

Canned Dog Food

Dog food in cans has become popular since World War II. Cans are convenient to buy, store, and use in small amounts. Canned dog food is also highly palatable (largely because of high moisture content). Convenience and palatability are the strongest advantage of canned dog food.

Canned dog food disadvantages are several. It is the most expensive way to feed a dog. The high moisture content (sometimes over 80 percent) can lead to rapid spoilage, even at room temperature. Canned food may contribute to loose and smelly stools. A steady diet of canned food may also promote teeth problems.

Many dog breeders use canned products as "mixers" with dry food as one way to encourage appetite. This use is probably preferable to straight feeding of canned dog food.

Semimoist Food

Semimoist dog food is a compromise between the convenience and palatability of canned food and the cost effectiveness of dry food. Usually marketed in burger or other "meaty-looking" configurations, semimoist dog food, while more palatable than dry food, sacrifices something in stool firmness and in economy. Moisture ratings are generally around 30 percent for semimoist foods.

These "in-between" foods are useful on trips and at those times when your dog's appetite may

Feeding Your Keeshond

be a little sluggish. Semimoist dog food is not widely used by show dog breeders; the majority of its sales are in grocery stores.

Dry Dog Food

Easily the most popular form of dog food, the dry form has many advantages. The most important advantage is the availability of a number of nutritionally complete and balanced dry foods. These have a lot to offer your Keeshond.

Dry dog foods store well without refrigeration. They are really good for your dog's teeth; harder, crunchy foods actually help remove tartar and promote clean teeth and gums.

Dry dog food's only disadvantage is less palatability, and this is not a major issue if you feed a premium brand, which has sufficient fat to make it tasty and appealing. Stool quality with a premium dry food is usually much better than with either canned or semimoist types.

In feeding dry dog food always remember that such food has only about ten percent moisture. Plenty of good, clean water will be especially important. Make sure that your Keeshond's water bowl is always filled.

Homemade Diets

As a rule, unless you can legitimately call yourself an expert in canine nutrition, avoid homemade diets. There are so many good, nutritionally complete, and balanced commercial dog foods that homemade dog food is generally not only unnecessary, but, unless you are expert, possibly risky for your dog.

Another word about table scraps. Human food is designed for human digestive systems and normally cannot be easily digested by your dog. Your dog deserves a nutritionally complete canine diet. Not only are some human foods, like chocolate, dangerous for dogs, but the more table scraps you

give your dog the more the chance for obesity—a real killer of pet dogs. Table the scraps!

Treats

Treats for your dog should complement, not undo, the balance of its regular food. Premium dog biscuits (available at the same places as premium dog food) will help you avoid any dietary imbalance for your Kees. These biscuits will serve as treats, rewards, and training aids. Overall formulation of the biscuits should blend with your dog's food.

Other dog items, like rawhide and nylon products and sterilized cow hooves are more useful for chewing rather than as treats. These chew toys help puppies' teeth and prevent destructive chewing behavior.

Feeding Puppies (One Year Old and Younger)

Your Keeshond puppy needs and deserves the best possible nutritional start. This start will require not only a complete and balanced diet, but the added nutrition that growing and developing puppies must have.

A good rule of thumb is that pups need twice as much complete nutrition as do mature dogs. After consulting your veterinarian, find the puppy food that best meets the dietary needs of your Kees pup and stick with it.

Initially your puppy will need three or four meals each day. At about six months of age, your Kees can be cut back to two feedings per day (depending on the maturation of this particular puppy). Of course, without excellent puppy food you won't be doing the best you could for your Keeshond, no matter how many feedings you give per day!

Feeding Your Keeshond

Feeding Adult Dogs (Over One Year Old)

Physical maturity for a Keeshond is achieved at around eighteen months to two years of age. With this next phase of your dog's development, its nutritional needs will change from those of a growing puppy to those of an adult Keeshond.

Your adult will still need excellent food to help it produce the lush Keeshond coat and to function well every day. Of course, a show or a breeding dog will need a diet more geared to the added stress of exhibition or reproduction. It is, however, important not to neglect the quality of the food fed to an ordinary pet Kees not slated for the show ring or breeding pen.

Your active Keeshond will need a good diet to power the dog into young adulthood, through its middle years up to oldster status at about eight to nine years. If your male Kees has been neutered or your female has been spayed, the nutritional needs normally are much more like the needs of older dogs.

Feeding Older Dogs (Eight Years Old and Older)

Metabolic changes in older Keeshonden usually call for corresponding changes in diet. As the systems of the dogs slow down, the need for energy producers in dog diets is lessened. Reduced amounts of fat and protein are common in the dog foods designed for the "senior" market.

Many pet dog owners fail to recognize the need for less fat and protein in their older dog's life. Patterns of feeding developed over the years die hard. Sometimes one will hear a Kees owner say, "Matty always eats two full bowls of dog food every day." The fact that Matty is now twelve years old and overweight has been overlooked.

Dog owners need to keep in mind that an obese dog, no matter how wonderful a pet it may be, will not normally live as long as a dog kept at an appropriate weight for its age. Use your resource team of veterinarian, experienced Keeshond breeders, and knowledgeable pet store personnel to assess the current dietary requirements of your Kees. You might also utilize the toll-free numbers of the dog food companies to get information about light dog foods or feeding strategies targeted at older dogs.

Some older dogs (as well as younger ones) may experience dietary difficulties, like allergies. They may need special diets. In such situations, your veterinarian is always your best source of information and treatment.

Shifting From One Dog Food to Another

While changing dog foods should never be undertaken impulsively, there may be times when a change is necessary. Gradual change is always preferable. One good way to switch foods is to use the "decreasing/increasing percentages method." (This method can be used not only to change brands but to move older puppies from puppy food to adult food.) For several days you feed 75 percent of the old food with 25 percent of the new. For two more days feed 50 percent of each food. Lastly, for several days (or until the old food is gone), feed 75 percent of the new food with 25 percent of the old.

Note: Some breeders use a variation on this method, making the feeding transition over the period of four weeks. The 75 percent old food/25 percent new food phase goes on for the first week. The 50/50 phase last during weeks two and three, with the 75 percent new food/25 percent old food continuing for the last week. Advocates suggest this longer way is a better way.

Your Keeshond and Medical Care

Keeping Your Keeshond Healthy

The best medical strategy in dealing with illnesses, injuries, and other health concerns is prevention rather than subsequent treatment. A strong preventive focus on your part will be far less costly and certainly far less uncomfortable for your Kees. Good preventive care centers on these common sense ideas:

- Avoidance of situations and conditions where there is potential for physical injury
- A nutritionally balanced diet and plenty of clean, fresh water
- A plan to keep your Keeshond as free from parasites (internal and external) as possible
- Regular exercise
- A safety-first attitude (using a leash when outside a fenced area, *never* leaving your dog in a parked car on even a moderately warm day, and so forth)
- Regular visits to the veterinarian for your Kees' checkups and appropriate preventive care
- The establishment of a health team for your Keeshond

Health Team

You and your family will obviously be the primary members of the team. You will be responsible for maintaining a safe environment, providing nutritious food and exercise in the right amounts, and arranging regular medical visits.

Your veterinarian will naturally be a key member of this team. He or she will help your Kees pup get a good start and help it through adulthood and old age. Nobody is better trained or more knowledgeable about how to keep your dog healthy than its regular veterinarian. Use this key resource person before problems arise, not just in medical emergencies. Establish a good communicating relationship with this veterinarian; your pet's health and life will certainly depend on it!

An experienced Keeshond adviser should be a team member. Experience with dogs in general and Keeshonden specifically can make this person invaluable. Your friend (as will the veterinarian and possibly the dog's groomer) will see your dog often enough to know it well, but infrequently enough to spot any subtle changes that may be the warning signals of a health problem.

A groomer could be a good member of your dog's health team. Each session gives an opportunity for an alert groomer to spot possible skin conditions, small injuries, and other small signs that might have a big impact on your Keeshond's health.

Preventive Care for Your Keeshond

A strong emphasis on avoiding health problems before they start, in combination with regular veterinary visits, will be the basis of a preventive care program for your dog. Not only will you lessen the chances of debilitating injuries and diseases (and the expense of such health problems) but your Kees will live a longer and healthier life.

Regular visits to the veterinarian will serve as an "early warning" system, not only alerting you to existing health concerns but to the possible problems you and your pet could have to face in the future. Your veterinarian will also keep your Keeshond vaccinated against a number of canine diseases. These immunizations are usually required by law, but also constitute good preventive health care.

Immunizations

Your Keeshond will have received the first of its immunizations while still at its breeder's home. Since you have carefully chosen the source from which you purchased your puppy, made cer-

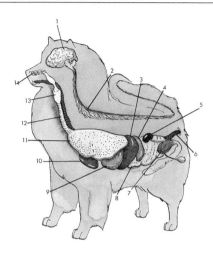

The major internal organs of the Keeshond:

1. Brain	8. Intestine
2. Spinal cord	9. Liver
3. Stomach	10. Heart
4. Spleen	11. Lung
5. Kidneys	12. Trachea
6. Rectum	13. Larynx
7. Bladder	14. Nasal sinus

tain to get the puppy's shot record, and made the acquaintance of a good veterinarian *before* you brought the puppy home, you know what immunizations have been begun.

Initial shots include the first in a series of inoculations against distemper, parvovirus, hepatitis, leptospirosis, parainfluenza, coronavirus, and bordetella. Six weeks of age is the appropriate time for these first shots, with some follow-up usually at eight to ten weeks and additional shots for some immunizations at twelve weeks. Develop an immunization calendar for your puppy with the help of your veterinarian. The calendar should have the dates and times for set appointments for these important protective shots for your puppy. Establish such a calendar and then strictly adhere to it! The best dog doctor in the world cannot help your puppy if you forget or neglect to take the puppy to your veterinarian's office.

The Diseases Controlled By Immunizations
Distemper

One need only read dog breeders' accounts from before World War II to discover what a widespread, highly contagious, and complete killer distemper was and can be. Distemper would hit a kennel and infect and kill all the puppies and most of the young adults.

Canine distemper, as a viral disease, would show up rapidly—approximately a week after exposure to an infected dog. Distemper can be characterized by a number of symptoms, but often would seem just a cold with fever and nasal discharge. A puppy or young dog would appear worn out and tired. Appetite would become almost nonexistent, with diarrhea also often present. Old-time dog breeders called distemper "hard pad" or "hard pad disease" because of a thickening and rigidity in the toe, foot, and nose pads.

Distemper would often throw a cruel twist at its unfortunate victims. Dogs would appear to be getting better, almost to the point of recovery, when the disease would resurface. The latter stages of this dread disease would include spasms, convulsions, paralysis, and, ultimately, death. Fortunately, modern veterinary medicine provides a vaccination that has greatly reduced the incidence of this killer distemper.

Rabies

Just the mention of the word "rabies" used to produce nightmare visions of "mad" dogs foaming at the mouth.

While your Keeshond may be a house dog or an apartment dog, you must be certain it has current rabies shots. If, for example, your dog was not immunized for rabies and came in contact with a rabid animal (an alley cat, a mouse, or even a squirrel) your best friend could, unintentionally, become your worst enemy.

Rabies can take on one of two appearances. There is a ferocious version that has a dog attacking everything around it, even cars or trees. The second form is a more lethargic expression of the disease, in which the dog is listless, slowly becomes comatose, and then dies. In both forms, a fear or avoidance of water has become a well-known symptom. Even an extremely thirsty rabid dog will not drink water.

Rabies can be prevented thanks to periodic inoculations, but only if dog owners like you provide this protection to your dog.

Leptospirosis

Leptospirosis is like rabies in one respect—it too can be transmitted to humans. Leptospirosis is a bacterial disease most commonly spread by drinking water that has been polluted by urine from an infected mammal. Exposure to a dog with the disease is another way it can be spread.

Symptoms of leptospirosis are loss of appetite, fever, vomiting, and diarrhea. Advanced cases show severe liver and kidney damage with attending jaundice. Abdominal pain, mouth sores, and a lack of strength in the hindquarters can also signal leptospirosis. Preventive immunizations are essential.

Parvovirus

Parvovirus is a very serious disease. It attacks the intestinal tracts of canines and can mean death for an unvaccinated animal of any age. It is a brutal killer of puppies up to four months old. A general lethargy, loss of appetite, vomiting, and sometimes bloody diarrhea are all parvovirus symptoms. Puppies with this disease often suffer from severe dehydration. Unless given immediate veterinary care, dogs and pups with parvovirus will die.

You can avoid this killer by a good vaccination program and a liberal dose of good judgment. View any stray or unknown dog that your Kees might encounter as a possible parvovirus carrier. If you can't be certain that a dog met on a walk or in the park has had parvovirus immunizations, you should assume the worst and protect your dog or puppy with the appropriate parvovirus vaccination.

Hepatitis

A dog or puppy of any age can be attacked by infectious canine hepatitis, a viral disease that can range from a moderate sickness to a deadly infection. In the latter form, infectious canine hepatitis can kill a dog within 24 hours of the onset of symptoms.

Hepatitis is characterized by abdominal pain, lethargy, vomiting, internal hemorrhaging, and tonsillitis. Immunization is an initial shot, followed by annual boosters. **Note:** Infectious canine hepatitis is not the same disease as the hepatitis that affects human beings. The canine version is not contagious to people.

Parainfluenza

Don't underestimate parainfluenza, the so-called "kennel cough." This is a highly contagious viral disease that can spread like wildfire through a kennel or wherever several dogs live in relatively close proximity to one another.

Parainfluenza produces tracheobronchitis—a dry, hacking cough followed by retching in an effort to expel throat mucus. By itself, parainfluenza isn't the worst or most likely fatal ailment to attack dogs, but it can leave a victim in a greatly weakened state—thus vulnerable to secondary infections and respiratory illness.

While you could separate a dog infected with the misnamed "kennel cough" from other dogs and lessen the impact of the infections, the best course is prevention by immunization from your veterinarian.

Bordetella

A bacterial infection, bordetella is often associated with tracheobronchitis (see Parainfluenza). As with other infections, the best treatment for bordetella is prevention. Immunization will control this and any accompanying tracheobronchitis.

Coronavirus

Dogs not vaccinated against this contagious disease can be affected at any age. Because this disease looks a lot like parvovirus, accurate coronavirus identification should come from your veterinarian.

Severe diarrhea characterized by foul-smelling, loose stools (sometimes tinged with blood) can be an indicator of coronavirus. Your Keeshond should be protected from this debilitating ailment by vaccinations; your veterinarian can best treat coronavirus in any dog not immunized. Don't waste time trying to decide which virus it might be (parvovirus or coronavirus); get a dog with these symptoms to the veterinarian promptly!

Lyme Disease

This well publicized ailment is another canine malady that can attack humans. Lyme disease can be transmitted even to dogs that spend only a small amount of time outdoors. City parks, suburban backyards, interstate rest areas all could harbor the tiny deer tick that causes this serious and sometimes fatal sickness.

While medical advances are still being made, your dog can be immunized against Lyme disease. You, on the other hand may not be so immunized. Catch any tick that may have bitten you and promptly have it identified by your family physician. If you only discover what could be a tick bite, a red area with a center like a bull's eye on a target, you would be well-advised to see your personal physician for verification.

Note: Veterinary medicine is progressing faster than books can be published. Your best bet in all immunizations is to faithfully follow your veterinarian's advice. So many of the diseases that were such killers only a few years ago have become preventable by inoculation. None of these canine health advances will do your dog any good if it doesn't receive the immunizations now so readily available. You should see that it does!

Parasites
Internal Parasites

Worms in dogs and puppies can constitute a serious threat to the overall health of your pets. Follow the advice of your veterinarian who will first discover what worms are present and then develop a treatment regimen to eliminate them. Regardless of what anyone says, treating your dog for worms is your veterinarian's role. Not only does he or she have the necessary diagnostic knowledge and skills, but your veterinarian will know the best eradication measures. Be concerned, be involved, but be wise and leave this job to your dog's doctor.

The possibility of worms in a dog's system, even in a dog that is primarily an inside pet, is another good reason for regular, periodic checkups. If you suspect your Kees may have worms at any time, get the dog and a stool sample to the veterinarian and begin treatment right away. Worms are parasites in every sense of the word. If your dog is infested with them, it cannot be at its healthy best.

Worms are usually found by detailed blood or stool examinations with a microscope. The most common worms afflicting canines (including your pet Keeshond) are roundworms, hookworms, tapeworms, and the potentially deadly heartworms. Each of these nasty critters requires a specific-veterinarian-approved treatment plan.

Roundworms: Roundworms can be found in dogs of any age, but most often in puppies. Puppies generally get roundworms from their mothers (if she has them) before the puppies are born or shortly thereafter.

Roundworms simply will not allow an infested puppy to thrive. Puppies with these parasites will not look as good as uninfested pups. They may have pendulous abdomens, or potbellies. Infested puppies may vomit up roundworms or pass them in their feces. After a routine stool exam, your veterinarian can begin to get rid of roundworms in the pups.

The flea is a pest that can spread another pest—the tapeworm. Fleas can be infested with tapeworm eggs. When the dog swallows an infested flea, the eggs are passed on to the pet to mature in the dog's intestines. Tapeworms can also be found in raw fish and raw meat.

Keeping the whelping box and all areas to which the puppies have access really clean is a good way to help prevent most parasites, including roundworms. It is especially important to keep the area as free as possible of any fecal material.

Hookworms: Hookworms, like roundworms, can infest dogs of any age. Puppies, however, are especially susceptible to these bloodsuckers that attach themselves to the small intestines of afflicted animals. Hookworms quite often can bring about anemia, sometimes fatal. Puppies with hookworms will not keep weight on and do not eat as they should. These pups may have either dark, tarlike, or bloody stools.

As with roundworms, keeping the puppy area clean is important. As important is the need for quick veterinary diagnosis and treatment.

Tapeworms: That age-old nemesis of dogs, the flea, is the usual transmitter of tapeworms. While tapeworms rarely do great damage to your Keeshond, the presence of these flat, segmented parasites is still a health problem for your dog.

Listen to your veterinarian, who will institute a treatment plan to eliminate the tapeworms. Your veterinarian can also advise you how to eliminate fleas, the host of the tapeworm eggs, from your home environment.

Heartworms: Another carrier-parasite brings this killer to your dog—the mosquito. If a mosquito infested with heartworm larvae bites your dog, it passes the larvae into your dog's bloodstream and ultimately into its heart.

While heartworms have been a warm region problem in past decades, they have become much more widespread in the past few years. To deal with these deadly invaders you must initiate early and faithfully follow a prevention course.

Your veterinarian can help you obtain preventive medication, which must be given on a regular, timely schedule. Without the preventive medicine, an expensive, prolonged, and somewhat dangerous treatment regimen will be necessary to prevent heartworms from clogging your dog's heart and bringing an early and miserable death.

External Parasites

Fleas: The most common parasite to afflict dogs, fleas, feed on your dog's blood, make the dog itch and scratch, and in some cases even bring on anemia. Fleas, as mentioned earlier, are also responsible for introducing tapeworms into your dog's system.

Some Keeshonden may develop a serious condition known as "fleabite allergy." This allergic reaction makes a common parasitic pest into a physical nightmare for the afflicted dog. Hair loss, skin problems, constant scratching, and general discomfort are symptoms of this extreme reaction to fleas. Your dog's doctor can provide not only a confirming diagnosis of fleabite allergy,

Possessing both beauty and brains, the Keeshonden are all-around athletes that handle both the physical and mental aspects of obedience training with characteristic vigor and good humor. Here an active Keeshond, jumps over an obstacle, and retrieves a training dumbbell.

but also prompt treatment to help alleviate this most miserable condition.

Fleas, even without severe allergic reactions in your dog (or perhaps even yourself), must be considered a major enemy. You must do everything in your power to eliminate fleas from every location in and around your home. Just spraying or dipping the dog is not enough. Fleas live, often for long periods, in rugs, shrubbery, beds, blankets, and cushions (in your house, in the dog crate, in the car, and so forth.) If you fail to diligently seek out and destroy fleas in all of your dog's environment, you will ultimately fail in your battle to rid your pet of these parasites.

Consult your veterinarian about "on-the-dog" flea treatments. You may have to consult your exterminator if your yard, house, or car become infested. Remember that fleas spend only about 10 percent of their lives actually on your dog. That leaves 90 percent of their lives to make yours very uncomfortable. Kill fleas *everywhere* they may live; it is the *only* way to control them. Always consult professionals when attempting to use chemical flea killers. If you do decide to use chemicals, follow all instructions carefully.

Ticks: Another external parasite that can attach itself to your Keeshond is the tick. Ticks are highly efficient bloodsuckers. Since they are much larger than fleas, they can consume much more blood. Ticks left undisturbed on a dog can become gorged on blood, growing several times their original size.

While bothersome and somewhat health-threatening (especially the tiny deer tick, carrier of Lyme Disease, see page 43), ticks can be handled pretty well with regular dips and sprays.

A Kees learning three key lessons: the "sit," which begins with the dog near the trainer's left foot (upper left); the "stay," which has the trainer presenting a palm in the dog's face while issuing the verbal command to stay (upper right); and the "down," in which the dog is taught to drop down on its chest and await the trainer's next instructions.

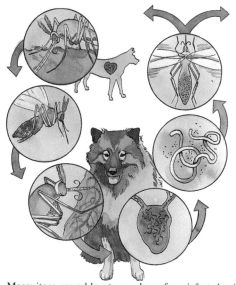

Mosquitoes spread heartworm larva from infected animals. Untreated, these larvae grow in the dog's heart and can cause great suffering and often fatal damage.

Never simply pull a tick off your dog. You will probably leave in your dog's skin part of the tick's mouth, which can become the cause of an infection. If you must remove ticks, follow the following steps:

• Place a drop of rubbing alcohol at the exact spot the tick has attached itself to your dog. Be careful around the dog's eyes!

• Using tweezers, carefully grasp the tick as close to the dog's skin as possible.

• Pull very slowly, making certain to get the entire tick, mouth and all.

• Put additional alcohol on the bite and dispose of the tick carefully to avoid its getting back on your dog, on another pet, or on you!

Always remain conscious that ticks can get on your housebound Kees from visits to wooded or grassy areas. A routine check of the dog's ears (a favorite hiding spot for ticks) and regular veterinary and/or groomer visits should keep these vampirish little creatures off your dog.

Ear Mites: Ear mites can cause a dog great discomfort. These microscopic mites live in the ears and ear canal. Their presence can cause a dark, waxy residue. Ear mites are easily transmitted to other pets (dogs or cats) and start a whole new infestation.

Symptoms of ear mites include dark waxy buildup in the ears, excessive ear scratching, and shaking the head from side to side in an often violent "no-no" type of gesture.

Again your best ally against this parasite is your veterinarian, who can rather easily identify and treat this problem.

Mange: There are two types of mange, both brought to a dog by mites. Red, or demodectic, mange, and scabies, or sarcoptic mange, are both skin conditions that need immediate veterinary attention. If left untreated, severe demodetic mange becomes a systemic disease that can be fatal. Good hygiene alone can prevent these diseases.

Red or demodectic mange especially affects old dogs and puppies. It causes ragged hair loss and sometimes is accompanied by itching, often severe itching.

Sarcoptic mange (scabies) is the result of mites that actually burrow into a dog's skin at the epidermal layer. They are highly contagious and can be easily transmitted from your dog to other pets or even to you. Sarcoptic mange also causes a lot of hair loss and a good deal of itching. To combat either mange see your veterinarian immediately!

Other Skin Problems and Conditions

Keeshonden, like other breeds, are sometimes the victims of a variety of skin problems—allergies, fungi, reactions. The already mentioned fleabite allergy is just such a skin problem. Some dogs may develop allergic reactions to certain foods or to some other aspect of their environment.

Some dogs are genetically predisposed to certain skin conditions. While most Kees have good skin, this is another reason for care in choosing the parents of your pup. Your veterinarian, so helpful with immunizations and parasitic conditions, can also be of great service with the diagnosis and treatment of skin problems.

One Keeshond feature that can complicate both external parasite and skin problem detection is the breed's thick double coat, which could hide parasites or problems. Unless you give your pet a regular going-over, you could miss the onset of some problem. Take time to check your dog thoroughly as often as you can.

Common Illnesses and Medical Problems
Vomiting and Diarrhea

Not all vomiting or diarrhea is a danger sign. Normally occurring events in a dog's existence can bring on either. Stress, diet changes (especially abrupt ones), and other ordinary happenings can bring on either vomiting or diarrhea. Puppies most often have these problems because of intestinal parasites.

But just because some vomiting and diarrhea are common, *never* ignore either. Both can be signals of other far more serious conditions. Any prolonged vomiting or diarrhea (more than a few hours) deserves a call or visit to the veterinarian. Until you are an acknowledged dog expert (by others as well as yourself) take all vomiting and diarrhea as possible indicators of serious problems and act accordingly.

Constipation

If your Keeshond has not been having normal bowel movements or is clearly straining when it does defecate, constipation could be the reason. Some constipation is brought on by changes in a dog's diet, traveling (especially when confined to its crate for extended periods), and other everyday causes.

If your dog yelps in pain while defecating or if constipation continues, a visit to the veterinarian is advised.

Impacted Anal Sacs

The anal sacs lie just under the skin on each side of the anus. Normally these are emptied of their strong-smelling secretions during ordinary defecation. Sometimes the anal sacs will become impacted (clogged). The sacs then must be emptied by hand. Your dog's veterinarian can show you how to do this admittedly less than pleasant, but very necessary task.

Evidence of impacted anal sacs could be a dog's "scooting" along the floor or yard, dragging its rear end. (This could also be a signal of tapeworm infestation.)

Gastric Tortion or Bloat

While Keeshonden are not particularly susceptible to this very serious medical problem, a knowledge of bloat could be important to any dog owner.

The specific causes of bloat have been long a partial mystery, even to professionals. Some breeds, and some strains (families) within a particular breed, seem to be more subject to bloat. Bloat involves the swelling of a dog's stomach from water, gas, or possibly both. The symptoms are:

- Obvious abdominal pain and swelling
- Excessive salivation and rapid breathing
- Pale, cool-to-the-touch skin in the mouth and gums
- An overall dazed look (as if the dog were in shock)

It has been thought that gastric tortion or bloat is associated with an overfeeding of dry dog food followed by a large amount of water and vigorous exercise. As stated, some breeds seem to be affected by bloat more than others. (Large and deepchested breeds and males over two years old seem to bloat more than females, other breed types, and ages.)

Bloat is a very serious condition. If your dog begins to exhibit these symptoms after a large meal followed by heavy exercise, assume the worst. *Rush this dog to the nearest veterinarian.* Bloat can kill a healthy, active dog in a matter of a few hours or less!

Inheritable Health Conditions

Keeshonden do suffer from some congenital maladies that also plague some other breeds. It is therefore possible to obtain a dog or a puppy with some inherited problems. You can largely avoid this by avoiding sellers who will not give you a "lifetime guarantee" that the dog is free from disorders that are passed along genetically.

Hip Dysplasia

One of the best-known (and worst) of these inheritable disorders is hip dysplasia or HD, a major cause of lameness in dog hindquarters. A dog afflicted by HD will not develop a complete hip joint. This makes walking increasingly painful.

HD is not normally diagnosed until a puppy has become a young adult. By the time this dread malady is recognized in your dog, you will have formed a bond with it and a return guarantee won't do your feelings (or the dog) much good.

HD is one of those concerns that are the reason for all that careful planning *before* you get your Keeshond. Insist on a puppy from parents that have been certified by the Orthopedic Foundation for Animals (OFA) to be clear themselves for HD and have healthy hips. If you can't get such assurance before you buy the puppy, look elsewhere.

Your Keeshond and Medical Care

Emergency Care
Accidents

Most accidents are preventable. Your Keeshond, after it gets past the puppy stage, should be able to stay pretty healthy in an environment where a little forethought has decreased the accident potential. But as careful as you may be, accidents do happen. There are some good rules to follow if your dog is injured:

- Don't make things worse, either for yourself or for the dog. Always muzzle an injured dog (even a normally loving Kees could bite its owner under such circumstances). You can make a muzzle out of a piece of cloth, a necktie, or a handkerchief, for example.
- Always handle the dog *slowly* and *gently*. You could fashion an emergency stretcher out of your jacket or shirt that will allow you to lift or move the injured dog without hurting it further.
- Always continue talking to the injured dog in a calm, reassuring manner.
- Call ahead and tell the veterinarian the nature of the injury and your approximate arrival time.
- Drive safely (and sanely) to the veterinarian's office. Make sure that an injured animal is not made worse by being tossed about in the car or by your stunt-driver turns.

The best way to handle all injuries (and diseases and parasites) is to prevent them. A key accident prevention rule that is the law in most places is "Never allow your dog to run outside without being under your control (a leash, a fence, or a confined area)."

Poisoning

Because your Keeshond lives with you in your home, there are any number of ways it can be poisoned by everyday items we often don't even recognize as dangerous. Perhaps the most insidious of these is ordinary antifreeze. Antifreeze is a triply dangerous substance: 1) It is a deadly poison to dogs; 2) it has a smell and taste that dogs adore;

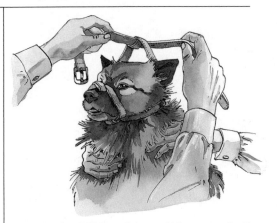

An injured and frightened dog could hurt you or itself. Using a belt, necktie, or something similar, gently put on a makeshift muzzle before attempting to move the pet.

3) it is in and around the family car, which is usually near the family and the family dog.

Chocolate is another poison that is an ordinary around-the-house item, but in sufficient amounts it can kill your dog.

Some house and yard plants are dangerous, especially to young, chewing puppies. Even such common favorites such as azalea, rhododendron, some hollies and other yard shrubs could prove toxic to your Kees. One dog owner was very careful to check out all house and yard plants for dangerous side effects only to have her dog become deathly ill from mistletoe that fell from a neighbor's tree into her dog's area. If you are not certain that the plants you have in and around your home are safe, contact your veterinarian or county extension service and make sure! Toxic house plants include poinsettia, dieffenbachia, and jade plant, among others.

Household chemicals can adversely affect your dog. Not only is your dog's head at the level where many substances are kept and used, but dogs are sniffers and lickers and can ingest toxic items you might not even realize.

If your dog begins to act listless, suffer from convulsions, disoriented behavior, vomiting, diarrhea, or a change in color of the mucous membranes, rush this dog to the veterinarian.

Bleeding

As a part of accident treatment, you may be called upon to aid your bleeding dog. Here are good points to remember:

- You would be wise to put on the aforementioned muzzle before beginning to stop bleeding.
- Find the source of the blood. If the bleeding appears to be internal, blood from the nose, mouth, ears, or rectum, transport the dog to the veterinarian immediately.
- If the bleeding is coming from a wound or an extremity (legs, ears, or tail) place a tourniquet between the injury and the dog's heart. Loosen this tourniquet for 30 to 60 seconds every 15 minutes.
- Continued bleeding, any significant blood loss, or a gaping wound will require prompt veterinary attention. As a rule, treat all bleeding as serious.

Heatstroke

Perhaps the most senseless way for a dog to die is because of the stupidity of an owner who left it in a parked car on even a moderately warm day. Your Kees can be dead or dying after just a few minutes in a car with poor ventilation on any day when the temperature reaches 60° F (16°C), even when some of the windows are left partially open. Never put your Keeshond in such a potentially deadly situation. This includes any enclosed area. Your Kees is an even more probable victim due to its thick double coat.

Heatstroke symptoms include rapid, shallow breathing with a high fever. The dog will have a dazed, "shocky" look and its gums will be bright red in color. *You must act immediately.* Lower the dog's temperature by applying cool water (or a mixture of cool water and rubbing alcohol) externally all over the dog's body. After lowering the temperature, rush the dog to the *closest* animal hospital or veterinary office.

Old Age and Your Keeshond

As a rule, older dogs (perhaps eight or nine years of age) will begin to slow down just a bit. As more years pile on, in most instances, you will begin to see your dog sleep a little more, play a little less, but still be a viable part of your home and your life.

There are a whole new set of health issues that can affect older dogs. Teeth and gum problems, bowel and bladder maladies, the beginning of a loss in hearing and eyesight are all areas of potential concern.

Good canine dental care (begun when the dog was a puppy) with a good diet will help allay many of the dental problems in aging dogs. Balancing diet and exercise with an appropriate weight should hold off some stomach and urinary tract concerns. Regular veterinary checkups and good routine care should give an ordinarily healthy Keeshond all it normally needs to age gracefully.

Health Areas to Watch
Teeth

During your Keeshond's entire life tartar accumulation on its teeth will be a concern. You can help lessen tartar buildup in part by feeding a good dry dog food that requires a lot of chewing and grinding. This basic canine eating action will help reduce some tartar, but you will need to see to the dog's teeth yourself by regular brushing to reduce tartar levels significantly. Start this regimen while your pet is still a puppy. Veterinarian-approved dog biscuits, nylon bones, and chew toys can also help with this problem.

Tarter buildup is a major canine tooth problem, but it can be made much worse by neglect. From puppyhood on make it a point to regularly

Your Keeshond and Medical Care

check your Keeshond's teeth, gums, and mouth. Because most Kees live close to their humans, obvious problems like bad breath are readily noticed. Tartar and other problems like early tooth decay or loose teeth will not be so easy to spot. Your veterinarian could make teeth cleaning part of each regular checkup. Combined with your diligence in taking care of this important canine health area, your Keeshond should have good teeth for most of its life.

Eyes

The eyes of the Keeshond are among its most captivating features. Large, prominently set, your Kees' eyes, while not normally a problem area in the breed itself, will need your preventive attention.

Especially in puppyhood, you should help avoid possible eye damage by keeping sharp objects away from puppy eye level. Because of its innate curiosity, a young Keeshond may not recognize sharp points as dangerous. You must help avoid eye injuries by assessing the dog's environment for anything that could hurt or irritate your pet's eyes. Sharp plants like flax or cacti are possible dangers. An angry cat could do eye damage to a puppy or young dog. Children throwing stones can hurt a dog's eyes. Attention on your part will help save your dog from eye damage.

Most other eye care will require just your good judgment. If your Keeshond begins to show discomfort with its eyes, or if the eyes are red, or have excessive discharge, take the dog for medical evaluation. As with sharp objects, eye irritants (auto emissions, air pollution, chemical fumes) can all bring on canine eye problems. Some dogs show a marked aversion to tobacco smoke. If your Kees goes through thickly wooded areas, possible mishaps or even foreign matter in the dog's eyes can result. Check your dog's eyes as often as you can. Early detection of eye problems (like cataracts in older dogs) can usually mean a successful medical outcome.

Regular checks of the dog's eyes (as well as ears and teeth) can help you identify any small problems before they become big ones.

You may notice on occasion some mucuslike material forming in the corners of your Kees' eyes. This happens to most dogs of all breeds and really isn't something to worry about. Gently wipe the matter out with a soft tissue. Don't confuse this ordinary mucus with an eye discharge, which should receive veterinary attention.

Ears

When you do your regular exam for ear mites you can also assess the overall ear health of your Kees. If you spot inflammation, discharge, or anything that doesn't look normal, get prompt professional care.

After each visit to wooded areas, you would be well-advised to check your dog's ears for ticks. These bloodsuckers especially like to hide in the recesses of a dog's ears. (For tick treatment see Ticks, page 47).

Nails and Feet

A regular part of responsible dog ownership is attention to the dog's nails and feet. Starting when

Your Keeshond and Medical Care

you bring your Kees home for the first time, you should keep its nails trimmed and give its feet a regular going-over.

By beginning nail trimming (as with teeth cleaning, brushing, etc.) while your Keeshond is still a puppy, you will teach the dog not to fear this very necessary and ongoing procedure. Even if your Kees spends a lot of time outside, running on hard surfaces that will help keep the nails worn down, you still should give the nails a thorough exam every week or so.

Trimming your dog's nails isn't difficult. Use a sturdy pair of nail clipper scissors or a "guillotine" type clipper, both of which are available at pet stores. The most important point to remember is that dog toenails have a vein inside, called the "quick," that will bleed if you cut off too much of the toenail.

Administering Medicine

You should know how to give your dog the prescription medicines that your veterinarian recommends for treatment and/or prevention of certain conditions. Some dogs don't like medicine and may spit out pills and capsules. No matter how good the remedy, if your dog doesn't swallow it, it won't do any good. A common way to get pills into the dog is to hide the capsule in some treat. Some breeders use a small piece of bread covered with peanut butter into which the pill is folded.

The most direct approach to giving pills is to open the Keeshond's mouth, tilt its head back a little, and place the pill as far back on the tongue as you can reach. Simply close the dog's mouth, speak reassuringly, and wait for the dog to swallow. **Note:** *Never throw the capsule or pill into the dog's mouth or tilt its head far back.* Doing either could cause the pill or capsule to go into the windpipe instead of down the gullet.

You give liquid medicines in a similar way, being careful not to tilt the head back too far. Sim-

ply pour the medicine into the pocket formed in the corner of the dog's mouth. Tilt back the head, stroke the dog gently under the neck, and speak in soothing tones while making certain that the animal swallows the dosage.

A final, but important, word on medicines. Always follow the veterinarian's explicit instructions on what, when, and how much to give.

Euthanasia

There is perhaps no sadder moment in the life of a dog owner than when the realization comes that age, infirmity, or terminal illness has robbed a pet of all of the things that made life a joy. That adorable Keeshond puppy so eager to learn will one day, barring a premature death, become an old dog slowed by the passing years.

It is never easy to recognize that a friend whose life has made yours so much better will be better served by a humane farewell. While this choice is certainly difficult, it is far better than allowing this good pet to live in constant suffering. For your once clownish Keeshond, whose antics brought so many smiles over the years, even the most basic daily activities become torturous.

When your faithful companion comes to these bad times, you should discuss matters with your veterinarian. If you have been diligent about your dog's health, the veterinarian will be an old friend of your Kees by now and may even love the dog almost as much as you do. This trusted and knowledgeable advisor will guide you in making this really tough decision.

Euthanasia, painful though it is for you to consider, is a painless procedure for your pet who can't understand why its life hurts so much now. In a real and loving way, choosing to help your pet get beyond its suffering is the kindest gesture you could make in payment for the long years of devotion that your Kees has given you.

Training Your Keeshond

Understanding Pack Behavior— The Key to Successful Training

You undoubtedly think of your Kees as a family member. You may not always remember that your dog is a member of some other groups. You probably know that Keeshonden as a breed are classified in the nonsporting group in the AKC and in several other kennel clubs. Your Kees is also a member of the canine family, and as such is naturally affected by the "law of the pack."

Your Kees, the huge Newfoundland, and the tiny Chihuahua are all pack animals. The concept of the pack and of pack behavior can be a natural and quite useful training aid. But to use pack behavior you have to understand it.

The pack is the most important factor in a dog's life. This canine caste system in the wild can regulate almost every facet of a dog's existence. In your home, you, your family, and other pets become a young Kees' "pack." Your dog will come already pack-conditioned by its mother and littermates. The mother dog, even in the puppy's short time with her, will have impressed on your Keeshond the rules that will determine its place within the hierarchy of the pack.

In the pack each member has its own place. This rank ordering is usually based on physical strength and knowledge (or "savvy"). In most packs the largest, smartest male fills the role of pack leader—the alpha male.

The alpha male takes charge of the group, resolves differences between pack members, helps keep younger members in line and out of trouble, and generally runs the show. The alpha male keeps this position only as long as he is strongest and smartest.

Within your home and within the life of your Kees, *you* will have to fill this role. The other members of your household will be the other pack members. You and your family will become a logical and important extension for your Keeshond, providing the security and sense of belonging that the pack offers. A well-adjusted dog needs an understanding of where it fits in its universe. You will have to assume responsibility for seeing that this chain of command is put in place and followed.

While instilling the pack concept is critical for your Keeshond, it is also very important to you and your family. The pack is not just some cruel system based on subservience. It is the reference point that engenders within the dog a sense of well-being. It is vital for you to remember that if you or someone of responsibility in your family does not assume the alpha male role, the job of boss, as far as the dog is concerned, the dog will take the job itself. One only has to see an aggressive, domineering dog, impervious to its owner's wishes and commands, to observe the pack concept gone wrong. Your Kees is a smart dog, and in the absence of alpha leadership it will feel it will have to fill the void. Do not let this happen. You are the master. The dog, as much as you may love it, must do what you want and what you allow it to do.

You will find training your dog much easier if you will follow the mother dog's approach and example in training her puppies. She instilled lessons that you can elaborate to help make your Kees the great pet and companion it should be. Her early training style took this form:

• The mother dog always treated each puppy in a litter *fairly*. She did not ignore puppy bad behavior, but neither did she overreact to it.

• The mother punished a disorderly pup *immediately*, while the puppy's short attention span could identify the misdeed with the subsequent reprimand.

• The mother dog reproved her babies *without anger*. She neither injured the puppy nor subjected it to incessant barking to correct its behavior.

• She treated the puppies in a *consistent* way. A misdeed was not ignored one time and then punished or rewarded the next time. Each puppy

Training Your Keeshond

was made to understand that certain bad acts drew punishment each and every time.

- The mother seasoned her reprimands with *love*. She gave her puppies the nurturing and place of security they needed. An earlier misdeed with its attending punishment did not banish the puppy from the warmth of mother and litter after the event was over. The mother did not withhold love as a way of enforcing her will.

A mother Keeshond will usually have laid an excellent foundation for the future training of one of her pups. By utilizing her style of fair, immediate, consistent response, without anger and in an atmosphere of love, you will find training your dog greatly simplified. Not only does this training style work, it is one which your puppy should already understand.

When to Begin Training

Some training, like housebreaking and basic rules of behavior, should begin as soon as your puppy comes into your home. Other serious training for your Kees probably shouldn't start much before six months of age. Of course some dogs will be ready for training earlier than others. Your dog's level of physical and mental maturity will dictate its readiness for training. Your Kees advisors and your dog's veterinarian will help you decide when your pup is old enough for lessons to be meaningful.

Note: Many approaches to dog training are based on simple lessons applied with great repetition. Your Keeshond may not adapt as well to this model as dogs of some other breeds do. As a bright dog, the Kees may grasp the task being taught quickly and then tire easily of the repetition. If you have never trained a dog and especially if you have never trained a Keeshond, you would be well-advised to seek help from an experienced Kees person. Training should be an enjoyable experience, and someone who thoroughly

knows the breed will be able to help you keep things both enjoyable and productive.

Essentials of Training

- **A Regular Time for Training Each Day:** These sessions should be free from distractions, short (not more than 10 or 15 minutes) and devoted to the work of training. Make them enjoyable but not centered on playing with the pup.
- **You are the Alpha Dog:** Be businesslike and consistent, with a stern voice. This will alert the puppy that training time is different from family time, playtime, and the other times you share with the dog. Remember the mother dog's lack of anger in her instruction.
- **A Clear and Realistic Training Goal:** Before you start a training session, have a clear and reasonable expectation for that session. A common fault of first-time dog trainers is to expect too much, too soon. Train in small steps and you'll be surprised at how far you and your Kees will progress. (A helpful hint: Discuss with your family what lesson you will work on each day. Make sure they understand what command you will be using. Encourage them not to confuse the puppy by undoing the lessons it learned during the session.)
- **Each Training Session As a Class:** Acknowledging that your Kees may not do well with rote repetition, it is still important to conduct each training time as a class. Each class should be short and have a single goal. Don't confuse the pup with several commands or activities.
- **Sticking to the Objective:** When you train, you can review previous sessions, but if the objective today is to teach sitting, focus on that goal. Correct your puppy *each* time it does not sit correctly and praise your puppy *each* time it does the right thing. If the dog begins to be bored with repetition, shorten the session. This does not mean that the dog does the command once

and then playtime begins, nor does it mean (especially for a Kees) continual and tiresome drilling.

- **Praise Used Appropriately:** While you love your dog and want to express that affection, use praise during training sessions as a reward for learning. You would do well to have a cushion of time between the training session and any subsequent playing. Make certain the dog knows that an enthusiastic pat for following a command is different from an affectionate hug at another time of the day.

- **Corrections Come Immediately:** Like the mother dog, you should make corrections right on the spot. Waiting to correct until later serves no useful purpose, since the dog will not remember what the correction is about; such belated punishment can only cause the dog to be and confused about what is good behavior.

- **Patience Important in Training:** Always remember that your Kees is, regardless of its good qualities, still just a dog. Your pup will want to learn the lessons you want to teach it. Be patient with this bright young dog. Adopt your training to the speed of the dog's learning.

Housebreaking

Because of the nearness to you of your Kees as a house dweller, one of the earliest and most essential lessons you will want your pet to learn is when and where to defecate and urinate. When this undeniable urge is combined with a great desire to please you, powerful forces are at work. You can use these forces to help the dog become an excellent household pet or you can try to go against them and get a dog that will never be housebroken.

Regardless of how much your Keeshond puppy may want to please you, it will have limited bladder control until it is about six months old. (Some dogs do mature more quickly). You begin the

housebreaking lessons by promptly introducing your new puppy to the place you have chosen for waste elimination and by lavishly praising the puppy for defecating and urinating at precisely this spot. But because of the age of the puppy, don't expect perfection until the pup's physical capacities mature. By no means does this mean that you wait four to six months to begin housebreaking, but don't be overly concerned if unavoidable accidents do occur, even after the young puppy seems to understand where it is to void waste.

Remember the cage/carrier/crate that was so important in providing a special den for your new puppy? This same crate will now prove its worth in the housebreaking process. Because of the pup's innate desire to keep its den clean, the crate is an excellent way to help the puppy begin waste control.

Crate training (See Crate Training Hints, page 58) will make the job of housebreaking a Keeshond easier. It will, however, require a careful plan regulating the timing of the puppy's feedings, with subsequent visits to the outdoor area for waste elimination. These coordinated efforts, combined with intelligent use of your dog's crate, and of course a lot of praise for the puppy when it successfully makes its pit stops outside, will work better than any other method in housebreaking your puppy.

For crate training to help you and your puppy, some understanding of when your puppy will need to defecate and/or urinate is necessary. After the puppy eats or drinks, the additional pressure on its bladder and colon will necessitate a trip outside. Be sure you remember to help your puppy by taking it to the appointed elimination site after each meal or drink. Another reason for such a trip could be a prolonged period of active play. Take the puppy out of its crate and outside as early in the morning as possible and also as late at night as you can. After the puppy has matured, the need for early morning and nocturnal elimination will lessen somewhat, but expect to provide relief trips for your dog in the morning, evening, and at other times during the day for its entire life.

Your puppy may try to tell you when it's time to go outside. Telltale signs are a general look of consternation, circling in one spot, sniffing for scent clues of where to "go," staying by the door, or whining and running toward the door to get your attention. If your puppy begins any of these behaviors, rush it outside. Even if the puppy can't wait and goes into a squatting posture in order to urinate or defecate, still make the effort to get the puppy outside. Do this in a calm, but rapid manner. When you pick up the pup, this will often surprise it and elimination may stop long enough to make the trip to the appointed location. Even if the puppy has an accident, if you get it outside and it defecates or urinates, praise the puppy lavishly. This praise, so important to the puppy, will reinforce the success of going in the right place.

Your behavior at the elimination spot is also very important. *Never* speak harshly or punish the puppy at this important spot. Your puppy needs a lot of successes (with the attending praise) to build and then reinforce the idea that outside is where defecation and urination belongs. Any negative influences at the place where praise is expected can only confuse a puppy who really wants to please you.

There will be elimination accidents with any pup. There are a number of things that you must not do if and when mishaps occur:

- Contrary to popular mythology, never rub the puppy's nose in excrement or urine. The puppy won't know what you're doing, and in addition, you'll have to wash the puppy.
- NEVER strike a puppy, for any reason, but certainly not for messing up in your house. Swatting a puppy with even a rolled up newspaper will do nothing but make the youngster fear and resent you.
- Shouting at a puppy is futile. You can break the puppy's concentration by clapping your hands and let it know it isn't doing the right thing by saying simply "NO" in a firm authoritarian (alpha male) voice.

In addition to planned feeding times and regular relief outings, you can help your puppy through housebreaking in several other ways:

- Always emphasize with praise the times your Kees pup does what it should, where it should.
- Feed a high-quality puppy food that emphasizes good digestibility. The stool with this type food will be smaller and firmer, an added benefit if an inside mistake does happen, and much easier for a young dog to "hold" than a food that contributes to a loose, runny stool.
- Never feed table scraps. Not only are they nutritionally unbalancing but they may actually bring on diarrhea and/or vomiting.
- Do not leave food out for your Kees puppy all day long. Not only does this throw off your planning for when to take the pup out, but your youngster will actually do better on three to four small meals a day.
- Never put food or food items (biscuits, edible treats, etc.) in the dog's crate. The puppy will

When walking your Keeshond out in public, keep the dog on a lead or leash. Always be a responsible dog owner and clean up any messes your pet may make.

not be able to keep its den area clean if bits of food are ever present.

- Methodically follow your feeding and outing plan and crate training. This method will work for you in housebreaking your Keeshond puppy.
- Discourage repeated inside messes by thoroughly cleaning up any that do happen. Deodorize the accident spots on the floor to prevent your puppy from catching its scent and repeating the act.

Paper Training

A less efficient and less effective way to housebreak your puppy centers on the use of newspapers spread around the floor in a laundry room or bathroom where the puppy is exiled if no one is home.

Crate training is so easy in most cases that even including a discussion of paper training might seem unwise. Unfortunately some lifestyles and circumstances make rushing a puppy out of its crate and then outside difficult. Some people must leave their puppy alone for several hours or all day. You could not very well leave a young pup in its crate for such extended periods without relief breaks. Also, some people live in apartments, and a rapid descent to the elimination area might not be easily accomplished. For these people, paper training is a slower, less efficient, but possible way to housebreak a puppy.

Paper training involves confining the puppy in some easily cleaned area. It does not work particularly well with crate training and hurrying outside because a puppy will be confused with two "right" places to defecate and urinate.

Some aspects of paper training are:

- Your puppy will need three distinct areas within the confinement room; (a) an elimination area, (b) a food and water area, and (c) a sleeping area containing the puppy's cage/crate/carrier.

- The elimination area should be covered with several layers of newspaper (printed with black ink only). The use of layers allows the top sheets to be used and removed, with the puppy's scent remaining behind on the subsequent layers to remind it where to go next time.
- Since almost all puppies will not want to mess up their eating and sleeping areas with feces and urine, these must be as far as possible from the elimination area.
- Whenever possible, reward the puppy's use of the elimination area with praise. Since the puppy cannot go outside as often in paper training, the praise may not have quite the same training effect as it would in the method using only outside elimination.
- You can combine paper training with the outdoors method by continuing to take the puppy out early in the morning, late at night, and whenever possible during the day. Naturally you will praise the pup each time it eliminates outdoors.
- A further way of combining efforts makes the inside elimination area gradually smaller until only a small place is used for relief. This small place, papers and all, is eventually shifted outside as the puppy matures. Some people even "salt" the outside area with urine-soaked paper or feces to encourage the changeover from inside to outdoors.

One final note about housebreaking. If you live in an urban area and your puppy's relief spot is in a public place like a city street, always be a responsible dog owner. Clean up fecal material left behind by your dog and always use areas off the sidewalks.

Crate Training Hints

Crate training works because your puppy, placed in its crate and left there, will make every effort not to foul the crate. The puppy probably learned this lesson from the best trainer it will ever have—its mother—who made messing up the whelping box by a puppy old enough to know better a major sin. Additionally, in the wild, canines are very reluctant to bring unwanted attention to their dens by allowing the scents of feces and urine to predominate. Crate training thus makes use of two very strong, primal influences that will help the pup know what to do, if you will only encourage it. The following hints will help you help your puppy:

- Always be both positive and realistic about crates and the ways they can make training easier. Remember humans may view putting a puppy in a crate as imprisonment, but for the well-adjusted puppy the crate is its comfort zone.
- When you purchase your Kees puppy's crate, remember it won't be a puppy for long. Buy a crate large enough for an adult Keeshond and let the pup grow into its den. Use temporary partitions to make the size of the crate the best size for the puppy. Placing a small puppy in a too large crate will encourage the puppy to develop an elimination area in a far corner of the crate. Avoid this by keeping the crate just big enough for sleeping.

As a "denning" animal, your Kees puppy will soon realize that its crate, cage, or carrier is its own special place. Crate training also greatly eases housebreaking.

- Place the crate in an out-of-the-way but not isolated part of your home. Be certain that this placement does not put the crate in areas where the room temperature is highly changeable or in a draft.
- Put the puppy in its den when it needs to rest and for the times you will be out of the house for a few hours. Always take the puppy outside immediately upon your return home. When the puppy relieves itself, praise it and go immediately back inside.
- Do not make getting out of the crate a reward. Don't praise the puppy (other than at the relief spot) for 10 to 15 minutes after it is let out of the crate.
- Keep a mat or an old towel in the crate along with a favorite toy to make the dog's den more homey.
- Do not put food or water in the crate. These have their appropriate place outside the pup's den.
- If the puppy whines or barks in the crate, use a firm voice, full of authority (alpha male) to quiet the puppy.
- Explain the reason for the crate to your family and make certain they all understand why it's used and why it works.
- When in training, always give the puppy a half hour "breather" in its den, after training, before removing the dog to play.

Basic Dog Training

When your Keeshond puppy has become housebroken, answers to its name, and seems to fit into the family rather well, you may think that further training is not a high priority in your busy schedule. You may want to rethink this; even some general training can give your bright Kees an even better start as a pet and as a companion.

Training Your Keeshond

As has been previously mentioned, the teaching of a Kees requires a somewhat different approach. Because of the Keeshonden's natural intelligence stemming from long association with humankind, you will want to get the advice and assistance of someone experienced with Kees to help you in teaching your dog. You may be fortunate enough to find a dog trainer or training class with leaders who know this breed. If not, contact your Kees advisor or the breed club (see Useful Addresses and Literature page 77).

Training Equipment

Because of the thick ruff around the Kees puppy's neck, you can begin initial training with a flat or rolled leather collar and advance to the "choke" chain when the dog has matured. Don't let the "choke" chain name lead you to believe it is a cruel or hurtful device. This collar does not choke; it restrains. When your dog's attention is required or correction is needed, a quick short jerk on the leash attached to collar (accompanied by a stern "No") will get the dog's attention and serve as correction. This collar should be large enough to slip over the dog's head but with about an inch (2.5 cm) clearance and no more. Some people try to use adult-sized training ("choke") collars on puppies. A danger exists with the looseness of such outsized collars. It is also important not to leave the training collar on the dog all day. It can catch on something and a possible injury to the dog can result.

With the training collar you will need a leash, preferably leather, web, or nylon measuring 6 feet (2 m) long. This leash (or lead) will need to have a swivel snap at one end for fastening to the ring on the training collar. The other end of the lead should have a comfortable hand loop.

Thoroughly familiarize your young dog with the lead so that it will be comfortable when the lead is attached to the training collar.

The Five Key Commands
Sit

Most pups already know how to sit down. The essence of teaching this command is to get the pup to sit when and where you choose. The "sit" is also a good basic skill that you can return to in order to give a young pup a training success at the end of each training session.

With your pup's training collar correctly attached to the lead, maneuver your puppy until it is on your left side next to your left leg. Take up all but about 12 inches (30 cm) of the lead and hold the lead in your right hand. In one continuous motion, gently but firmly, pull up on the lead (thus lifting the dog's head) as you put gentle downward pressure on the dog's hindquarters with your left hand, saying as you do so, "Sit" in a firm voice.

Do not use excessive force to push the puppy's rear end downward. You only want the pup to sit, not to hurt it. An alternative to pressing down on the hips would be to use the same upward pull on the lead, but change to a gentle chopping motion *behind* the dog's hind legs. This action will cause it to sit down, as will the first technique.

Regardless of which version you use, be consistent. When the puppy does assume the sitting position, be lavish with your praise. Let the puppy know that it has really done something good by obeying your command. Associate in your dog's mind the command to sit with the action it took and the reward of praise it subsequently received.

Repeat this simple exercise several times, remembering to do all three components (the head lifting, the rear end lowered, and the command "Sit") the same way each time. The uplifted head will keep the sit from becoming an outright belly-flop. Your bright Kees puppy should soon readily understand this command and be sitting on its own when the command to sit is given. As always, praise is crucial every time a puppy successfully completes what you command it to do.

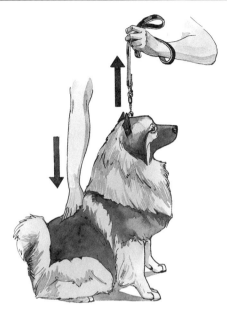

As the "sit" command is given, press downward on the dog's hindquarters while gently pulling up on the lead with the left hand.

Remember that excess repetition can lead to boredom or even resentment in some dogs. Keep training sessions brief. Always follow the same training steps each time. Don't initially try to leave a youngster in the sitting position for long periods.

Stay

The "stay" is best taught after the "sit" is well learned. The stay starts with the sit, and unless the puppy knows the first lesson, efforts at teaching the second will be futile.

For the stay, your dog again starts off on your left in the ordinary sitting position. Use the lead in your right hand to continue to keep the pup's head up. Using a command voice you say "Stay." As you issue the command you step away from the dog, making sure that you move your right foot first. As you begin to step away,

bring the palm of your left hand down in front of your Keeshond's face in an upside down version of the traditional police hand signal for "stop." The "stay" thus requires four actions on your part, all performed simultaneously and done the same way each time:

1. You exert gentle pressure to keep your dog's head up (as in the "sit").

2. You step away, leading with your right foot.

3. You put your left hand, palm toward the dog, in front of its face.

4. You give the vocal command to "stay."

At first your puppy, who naturally wants to be right with you, may not remain in stay for very long. Praise the puppy for any length of stay, but if it moves toward you, start over and do the command again. Your Keeshond should

The "stay" begins with your Keeshond in a "sit." The command "stay" is given as you step away from the dog (leading with your *right* foot). As you do this, bring the palm of your *left* hand down and in front of (but not touching) the dog's face.

come to recognize the hand in its face as a sign for it to remain in position. This recognition will be reinforced by the command to stay and by the praise the pup receives when it does the right thing. As with other commands, don't overdo the repetitions. If your puppy has trouble understanding what you want, after a few tries go back through a command it has mastered — the "sit" — and let the session end on a positive note with the puppy being praised for doing the sit correctly.

After your puppy has mastered the "stay" you will want to introduce a release mechanism, a signal that it can now come to you. Most trainers use a simple "okay" to let the pup know it can come back to you from the stay.

Heel

Your puppy has now learned to sit and to stay; now you need to be able to put some controlled movement in its life. The "heel" begins with your Kees in sitting position on your left. The pup's head should be in line with the placement of your left foot. Using your by now well-developed command voice, you add the dog's name to this command, as in "Matt, heel." The lead is attached to the training collar and again held in your right hand. As you give the command you step out, leading with your left foot. If the pup doesn't step out when you do, pop the slack in the lead sharply against the side of your leg and continue to walk. The absence of the restraining hand of the "stay" and the gentle pressure to go forward from the lead should do the trick. When the pup catches up with you, give it praise, but don't stop walking. Teach the pup that it will continue to get the praise only as long as it walks right by your side.

If your puppy doesn't get the "heel" concept immediately, don't drag the puppy along behind you just to cover some ground. Go back to sitting and stay position and start again. Keep the pulling pressure of the lead constant as you patiently but firmly encourage the puppy to walk by your side,

The "heel" command begins with the dog in a sitting position. Holding the lead in your *right* hand with the dog on the *left* side, train your Kees to walk along beside you.

at the correct position, stopping when you stop, turning when you turn.

When you do stop, give the "sit" command. The puppy should pick up the "heel" quickly because it wants to be with you anyway, but make certain that it stays in line with your left leg. Teach the command correctly and then correct the dog if it tries to walk in front of you or way behind you. You, as alpha dog, will decide where you two will walk. If the pup has trouble, don't become overly concerned, simply start again. As with most lessons, patience will ultimately make your puppy successful in accomplishing the "heel." Remember to end training time with a command the puppy knows and does well.

The Keeshond, was once known as the "Dutch barge dog," the "fox dog," and the unflattering "overweight Pomeranian." Recognized for centuries as a dog of the common people of the Netherlands, the Keeshond has been accepted by the various kennel clubs only since the 1920's.

Training Your Keeshond

Down

"Down" can be taught after the "sit" and the "stay" have been mastered. Starting in a sit, use the lead to exert downward pressure on the training collar and the dog's head in a motion just the opposite from that of the lead in the sit. Using your right hand, pull down on the lead while presenting the palm of your left hand in a downward motion (not unlike bouncing an imaginary ball) as you give the command "Down." Be patient with the puppy, and once it has reached the down position with its stomach on the ground, reward the puppy with loads of praise.

As with sitting, the down is simplified by the fact that the dog already knows how to do it. As with the sit, it is your job to associate this known position in the dog's mind with the command "down" and the gentle but constant pressure the lead is exerting to bring the dog's head down.

Your ultimate goal is for the dog to hear the command, whether you are standing there lead in hand or not, and obey it, remaining in the "down" position until you give the "okay" signal for the down to end. In your early sessions, even after the puppy understands and obeys, don't leave (or attempt to leave) the puppy in the down position for long periods. Gradually lengthen the periods the pup stays in the position by practicing the command in several short, enjoyable sessions. As with the stay, your dog shouldn't move about while it is in the down. Correct the pup if it does move, praise it lavishly when it does not.

Come

The "come" command may seem to be an easy lesson to teach, but you want the puppy to

An excellent obedience dog and an attractive show dog, the Keeshond remains a "natural dog" without the fads and overly accented features that have been seen in some breeds. Even with a great deal of worldwide acceptance, the Kees remains pretty much what it has always been—a people's dog.

The "down" is taught by causing the dog's chest to go downward. The method shown is one way to move the dog from a sitting position.

know it must come to you without hesitation each and every time the command is given. To teach this command you will need enthusiasm, firmness, consistency. You should always call the dog by name, as in "Matt, come." When just starting, enthusiastically use your voice, spread your arms open wide and invite your puppy to come to be with you. When the dog does react immediately to this command, give it lots of praise.

One thing you must never do (or allow anyone in your household to do) is to call the puppy to you in order to punish or scold it. A puppy will associate the command with the fact that when it came to you, as you requested, something negative happened. If you want to correct a puppy for something it is doing wrong, go to the puppy and do the correction! You can teach the "come" while the pup is on its everyday lead, but you will definitely need a longer line to reinforce that the command means the dog is to come from far as well as from near. A lead of 20 feet (6.5 m) would not be too long. Use this lead to exert firm pressure for the dog to come directly to you when the command "come" is given. As with teaching the "heel," you do not want to drag the puppy all over the yard, but you do want to get and keep its

attention. A sharp tug on the lead can do just that. Always use your authoritative voice to emphasize that you mean business when you use the command "come." Praise becomes especially important when the pup comes as it should. The command "come" is potentially the most important command your dog can learn, for a dog that will not return to its owner on command is a dog out of control. An out-of-control dog is possibly an accident waiting to happen. For the dog's sake make sure the "come" is its best command.

As mentioned, Keeshonden may not need as much training repetition as some dogs in other breeds. The "come" is just such an instance where repetition can backfire on a trainer. If a trainer repeatedly calls the dog, the dog may become jaded at the request, even with its pats of reward. After your pup has learned this lesson, use the command in other lessons and even in moments not specifically dedicated to training.

Obedience Classes

You should, with patience, be able to teach these elementary commands to your Keeshond. You can also get help from a more experienced Kees person or you can seek organized dog training classes available in your home area. These classes are usually available through a local dog club or similar organization. You could take lessons from a professional dog trainer.

A well-groomed, well-trained Keeshond in the show ring is a truly memorable sight.

There are many other actions your Kees can learn beyond sitting, staying, heeling, lying down, and coming on command. You could find that you and your dog would enjoy actual obedience work. A large number of Keeshonden have excelled in the obedience ring. Talk with other Kees people about their assessment of your dog as a possible participant in further learning. Read as much as you can about training (some good books on the subject are list on pages 77–78). If attaining "higher education" seems like an enjoyable goal for you and your dog, you should certainly check it out!

Grooming and the Keeshond

Grooming and the Kees—An Overview

As with any longhaired breed, the Keeshond will look its best if regularly groomed. Your approach to grooming should however be both mental and physical. If you perceive grooming as just another chore, you'll miss out on the fun and the relationship building that grooming can bring to you and your Keeshond.

Grooming a Keeshond doesn't have to be the awesome undertaking that some might think. If you begin early with your puppy, brushing it and making grooming yet another enjoyable experience for both of you, you'll be better off and so will your dog.

Grooming will allow you a regular opportunity to give your pet a thorough external examination. You will lessen the amount of shed hair by regular brushing. You will soon gain confidence in your own ability to bring out the best in your Keeshond's appearance.

Grooming Equipment

- A "slicker" brush with fine, slightly bent wire bristles
- A "pin" brush with blunt metal pins set in a rubber base attached to a wooden or plastic handle
- A metal comb with teeth a medium distance apart
- A close-spaced comb with fine teeth, often called a flea comb
- Straight-blade scissors for trim work
- Nail clipper scissors (you could substitute the "guillotine blade" nail clippers here.)
- A spray bottle or atomizer for spraying the dog's coat with a fine spray of water

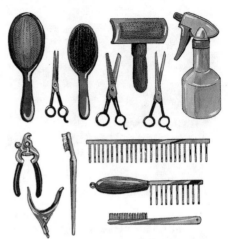

Keep your Keeshond looking good by regular grooming with the right combs, brushes, scissors, and a spray mist water bottle. Don't forget periodic tooth brushing and nail trimming.

Grooming Your Pet Keeshond

Grooming should always be done in enjoyable surroundings. Don't try to groom your dog and do other things at the same time. Find a sturdy, secure surface that will support the dog's weight. Pick an area where the inevitable product of grooming—loose and cut hair—can be easily cleaned up later.

You will need a spray water bottle to gently mist your dog's coat before actual grooming. Misting will reduce static electricity and make the job easier, with less damage to hair ends. After you have carefully cleaned your dog's face, ears, and eyes, briefly mist the dog with water, taking care not to hose the dog down with too much water.

Working slowly and gently, flatten a portion of the dog's coat; and using the pin brush next to the inner coat, brush outward toward the ends of the coat hair. You want to bring the Kee's coat outward and forward to frame the face and give

Grooming and the Keeshond

When brushing your Kees, always brush *away* from the dog and *forward* to make the coat and mane stand out in characteristic Keeshond style.

Bathing your Keeshond should not be undertaken too often. Frequent bathing could cause a Kees' coat to become dry, brittle, and dull. If your Keeshond cannot be cleaned by thorough brushing, use a quality dog shampoo. Follow the instructions and safeguards on the shampoo and be sure to thoroughly rinse the Kees' outer and inner coat of any shampoo or residue. Be careful. Don't allow shampoo to be swallowed or to get into the dog's eyes. Dry the dog thoroughly using a rough bath towel. You may find an electric hair dryer helpful, but excessive use can dry out the coat and skin.

the ruff the full, distinctive Keeshonden look. Groom each part of the body coat the same way, always brushing away from the dog and forward. Remember to start the brush down in the coat next to the skin and brush completely to the end of the coat hair.

Using the finer "slicker" or even the "flea comb," touch up the hair on the face and on and around the ears. You can also use the "slicker" to brush the dog's legs and feet.

Using your straight scissors, shape up the hair on the feet and legs. Do such trimming with great care and without overdoing it. You want just to make the legs look neater by trimming away hair that spoils the clean lines of the front legs and the charming "trousers" of the back legs. With extra care trim the hair on the sides and top of each foot, leaving a foot with a round shape.

Always keep your Keeshond's nails neatly trimmed. When trimming, always avoid cutting into the "quick"—the part of the nail that will bleed. Your veterinarian or other pet professional can show you how to do this needed chore safely and correctly.

Raising Quality Keeshonden

Reasons, Realities, and Responsibilities

Allowing a litter of Kees puppies to be born is a serious decision that should never be taken lightly. Casual dog breeding, without any thought to the future of the pups, is irresponsible at best and cruel at worst.

Cute puppies grow up to be adult dogs. They deserve every chance to belong to a home that really wants them and is able to provide competent care. If you are not ready (if necessary) to keep every puppy you allow to be born, you should not become a dog breeder. A responsible dog breeder will carefully plan each breeding to produce the best possible pups. The pups will be given the best possible start in life; they deserve nothing less.

A vital question to ask yourself before starting to breed dogs is "Why do I want to raise Keeshonden?" Perhaps the only legitimate answer is the desire to improve the breed. If you simply want to let your little Kees bitch experience the joys of motherhood, do her and yourself a big favor and skip it. If your Keeshond female is of pet quality, the chances are overwhelming that she will produce only pet quality puppies. In case you haven't heard, there are too many pet puppies out there already. Why would you want to add to the number when there are not nearly enough homes to go around?

If your reason to produce a litter is so your children can witness the miracle of birth, think again. After the miracle is long over the resultant puppies could live less than miraculous lives. Cute puppies have the annoying habit of growing up, first into awkward adolescents and then into full-fledged adults. Your children could gain experience with puppies by visiting a breeder and, under supervision, perhaps assist in socializing a litter of pups.

It is to be hoped that your motivation to breed Kees is not founded on some financial dream of wealth. Such an idea is nonsensical. Most dog breeders will tell you that they spend a lot more than they ever earn dog breeding. Even top show kennels rarely end up "in the black," even after years of careful effort.

If your wish to raise Kees stems from some ego need to be identified as a dog breeder, rethink this. Your ego would be better served by buying a great pup and then campaigning it to a championship.

You may find that aspiring to produce excellent quality Keeshonden puppies really does interest you. You should read, reread, and commit to memory the "Breeders Code of Ethics" (page 16). If after careful study you sincerely believe you can adhere to all the tenets of this code, you may have some reason for further consideration of Kees breeding as a primary interest. If your aim is to produce the best Kees possible, you may be on the right track in giving dog breeding further thought. One way to pursue this ambition would be to apprentice yourself to an acknowledged and willing Kees breeder. Before you ever breed your own dogs, talk with veteran breeders and learn how they make the numerous critical Kees breeding decisions.

After you have "paid your dues" and learned all you can, review your own situation. If producing a litter of Keeshonden puppies will stress your family finances, or if every family member isn't enthusiastic about this project, or if your living arrangements would make the possible keeping of all the pups impractical or impossible, perhaps the time is not right for this Keeshond breeding venture.

Have your Kees evaluated by an impartial third party for its breeding potential. One way of validating your Keeshond's genetic value would be to exhibit it to an American Kennel Club championship.

Your veterinarian should carefully examine your dog. An assessment should be made of your Kees' hips, eyes, and other potential problem areas that could signal a congenital defect that

might be passed on to offspring. Your veterinarian should also appraise your pet's overall general health. If any concerns arise after your veterinarian has checked out your Keeshond, you may want to relegate your dog to pet rather than breeding status.

As a final acid test, visit your local animal shelter, perhaps with your family. Look long and hard at the groups of adult dogs and puppies, realizing that the overwhelming majority will never be adopted. Consider what the alternative to adoption is in most of these shelters. Then decide whether you want to cause more pups to be born.

The Estrous Cycle

A Kees bitch will usually come into heat or season approximately twice yearly. This occurrence is known as the estrous cycle and should happen for the first time between six and eight months of age. Different bitches (and different breeds) may show slight deviation in timing.

Usually the estrous cycle is differentiated by several phases:

• *Proestrus*, or the preparation phase of the cycle, is identified by the beginning of activity in the uterus and ovaries. The ovaries start to produce eggs (ova). As these eggs mature, the uterus becomes thicker and a blood-colored discharge from the vagina can be observed. Proestrus usually lasts an average of nine days, although it may be as brief as four days or as protracted as nearly two weeks. Your Kees bitch will attract males during the proestrus phase, but will not be ready for mating. Additionally, the outer female genital organ, the vulva, will become somewhat enlarged.

• In the second phase of the estrous cycle—*estrus*—the observable vaginal discharge will lose some of the bloody color, becoming clearer and taking on a thin, mucuslike consistency. Your bitch will continue to attract male dogs, and during the estrus phase mating can actually occur. Ovulation takes place during this phase

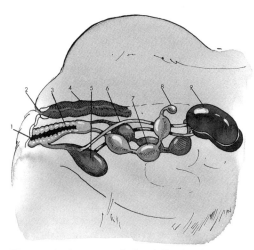

The reproductive system of a female Keeshond:

1. Vulva	5. Bladder	8. Ovaries
2. Anus	6. Ureter	9. Kidneys
3. Vagina	7. Developing	
4. Rectum	embryo	

and normally happens between the ninth and fourteenth day from the beginning of proestrus. Estrus will continue approximately the same length of time as proestrus. Conception is possible throughout the entire nine days (on average) of the estrus phase.

• Assuming your Keeshond bitch mated during the estrus phase, the *metestrus* will begin and continue for the next six to eight weeks. Metestrus is marked by milk production (lactation) preparation within the mammary glands.

• Metestrus ends as *anestrus* begins. Anestrus is the final phase of the estrous cycle, in which your Kees' uterus and ovaries begin to return to their preestrous cycle condition.

• If your Kees bitch does not mate she will gradually go "out of heat." Her vulva will shrink accordingly. Vaginal discharge will cease and her ovaries will cease to be active. This "out of heat" phase is her usual condition where she will remain for the next nearly half a year, when the estrous cycle usually starts all over again.

Raising Quality Keeshonden

Your bitch should probably be in her third heat before she is bred. At this time she ideally will be approximately eighteen to twenty months old.

Note: During the estrous cycle you should be ever vigilant to keep your Kees bitch away from all breeding age males. Failure to do so could easily result in an unwanted pregnancy. Constant chaperoning will be required anytime your female is out of a male-free home. Fences, at this stage, can generally not be counted on to stem the tide of romance. Your awareness and watchfulness usually can.

The Stud Dog

Your Keeshond female is only part of the equation for producing a litter of quality puppies. Not only should the chosen stud dog be a superior specimen in every way, it must have a pedigree compatible with that of your bitch.

Choosing a stud will require input from your experienced Keeshond breeder-advisers. Not only will these Kees veterans have an understanding of strains (families), but they may also help you make the right contacts with stud dog owners.

You have already had your female assessed by one or more Keeshonden breeders who will give you an honest critique. Assuming she has no outstanding flaws, she should be perceived by acknowledged experts in the breed as a bitch worthy of being bred—both physically and temperamentally. Your veterinarian has, after a thorough examination, certified that your Keeshond female has no obvious congenital defects or physical conditions to discourage her becoming a brood (breeding) bitch. The veterinarian has also given you a written statement that your bitch is free from the venereally transmitted, bacterial disease of brucellosis, which can wreak havoc with breeding dogs. Not only can this ailment cause aborted litters, but can leave adult dogs, male and female, sterile. Breeders who possess the quality stud dog

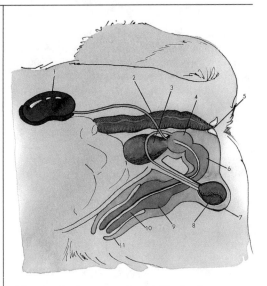

The reproductive system of a male Keeshond:

1. Kidney	5. Anus	9. Bulb
2. Rectum	6. Urethra	10. Penis
3. Bladder	7. Scrotum	11. Sheath
4. Prostate	8. Testicle	

you are seeking for your female will undoubtedly require this written clearance from your veterinarian before allowing a mating.

The stud service will probably not be free. You would be wise to have the stud fee (recompense for the male's mating with your bitch) clearly stated in writing, in advance. Quite often the male's owner will want a set fee and/or (if your bitch is of exceptional quality) choice of one or two of the resulting puppies. This "pick-of-the-litter" request is quite a compliment from a top stud owner, but you might be wise to keep the stud cost purely monetary. If you are serious about wanting to produce top-quality show puppies, you should realize that the pick-of-the-litter might well be the only puppy with show potential in the entire litter.

You have given the stud's owner your veterinarian's guarantee of the absence of brucellosis in your bitch. You should also receive a

guarantee from the stud owner that the mating will result in conception and in live puppies. If your bitch does not conceive, normally the male's owner will allow her to be mated again to the same stud at her next estrous cycle. This should be clearly understood in writing in advance.

If you do not know the stud dog owner well, you may want to be present when the mating takes place. You can be certain that the male you have chosen is the one that actually sires the puppies. While the vast majority of Keeshond breeders are ethical, your venture into dog breeding is new and you should take reasonable precautions.

A quality Keeshond male owner may, of course, refuse to allow your female to be mated with the stud dog. Don't misrepresent her as having show quality when she does not. A stud's owner knows that all pups sired by the stud become either good or bad advertisements for the breeding quality of the stud. The stud's owner also knows that breeding to a poor-quality bitch just for the stud fee is shortsighted. Poor-quality bitches almost always produce poor-quality pups.

Mating

You have done all your homework up to this point. Your Kees bitch is recognized as very good quality and worthy of being bred. She is temperamentally and physically sound. She has been wormed and her vaccinations are up-to-date. You may have placed her on a higher quality diet to enhance her conditioning. The pedigree of the stud is important, but the greatest Keeshond male cannot be expected to offset the negative impact of a poorly conditioned bitch.

You know that the ovulating phase of the estrous cycle is called estrus. You also realize that dog breeders try to introduce the male to the bitch on the ninth day of the cycle. While introductions may be in order, mating should take place shortly thereafter.

When copulating, the male and the female may be locked together or "tied." This is a natural effect of the interaction of the vagina and penis that will stop after several minutes. Your female may become tied with the stud more than once during the two or so days of maximum receptiveness. **Note:** A female in this stage of the estrous cycle could also mate with another male, even after the initial mating to the correct stud has taken place. Keep your female away from *all* other males until after the receptive phase is over. Failure to do so can cast serious doubt on the parentage of the pups.

False Pregnancy

Sometimes a female will fail to conceive (or never have been bred at all) and still show many of the external characteristics and actions of a pregnant female. This condition, false pregnancy, can be caused by certain hormonal problems or by ovarian cysts. Although accepted medical treatment may help, a bitch can develop pyometritis and related disorders that may require surgery for removal of her ovaries and uterus.

Pyometritis and other related problems occur most often in unspayed bitches that have not had puppies. Never ignore false pregnancy, for this may be a signal of more serious health problems. **Note:** If your Keeshond female is simply your pet and not a potential breeder, do her a real favor: have her spayed! Not only will you not have to face unintended matings with resultant unintended puppies, but she will be able to avoid many of the medical problems facing bitches.

Pregnancy

In most cases, gestation for canines is approximately 63 days from the time of the mating. At about the sixth week your Kees female will begin

to look quite maternal. Her abdomen will begin to get larger, as will her teats in physical anticipation of the arrival of hungry Keeshond puppies.

Your Kees mama dog will need even more attention and "TLC" than usual, especially if this is her first litter. Some breeders start her on a high-quality puppy food even before the pregnancy. She will, however, still need moderate exercise. You want her increased weight to be in Keeshond pups and not in fat; just don't let her overdo physical activity.

About fourteen or fifteen days before the puppies are scheduled to be born, you might be wise to separate the female from any other dogs you may have. Handle her with care during this time, avoiding any rough horseplay that might injure her. Let her have ready access to her den. Do everything you can to see to her physical and emotional needs—especially if this is her first litter.

The Whelping Box

Make absolutely certain that you are prepared for the impending birth of your Kees puppies. The whelping box, like the den, is a vestigial carry over from canine prehistory. This important place for whelping should be prepared well in advance of the event. The whelping box should be large

The Keeshond is usually a very good mother. Notice the well-constructed whelping box that keeps the puppies safe and gives the mother easy access to and from the box.

enough for your Kees bitch to lie comfortably on her side, as the box functions not only as a whelping area but must be the puppies' first home for several weeks.

Be sure to place the whelping box in a warm, dry place away from drafts and out of heavily traveled areas. Remember that your Kees mother dog needs a lot of your attention during this trying time, especially if this is her first litter. Visit the whelping box regularly and be especially tender with your female and her puppies.

A whelping box in a barn or shed should be up off the floor to avoid excessive coolness and dampness. The box should have sides high enough to corral young puppies and yet low enough to make entry easy for your Keeshond bitch with her now low-slung undercarriage. A shelf or rail several inches wide along the inside walls of the box will help keep puppies from being accidentally trapped and crushed by their dam's weight.

Also on the floor of the whelping box should be several layers of either blank newsprint or newspaper printed with only black ink. Avoid colorful advertising sections and the comic sections, as colored inks sometimes contain chemicals that could harm a newborn puppy. As the puppies mess up the top layer of paper it can be easily removed, leaving other layers still serviceable.

Preparation for Whelping

Your preparations have already begun with the building or purchase of the whelping box. You have also prepared for the upcoming births by marking off a range of possible whelping times on your calendar and have arranged to stay close to home for several days before and after the 63rd day. You have made being in attendance at the whelping a high priority.

Most Kees do not ordinarily have much trouble in birthing, but if this is your dog's first litter you don't know what may happen. You may want to

have your veterinarian on call and perhaps you can enlist the aid of an experienced Kees person who is well-liked by your dog. The watchwords are preparation and tenderness.

As whelping time approaches, your mother Kees will become increasingly restless and often quite anxious. Spend as much time as you can with her, constantly reassuring and praising her. By calmly showing your affection you will convey to her that all this strangeness will soon pass and that everything will be fine.

You should have already thoroughly discussed the impending births with your veterinarian, who can tell you what to expect, how to react, what constitutes a problem, and what to do about it. Don't hesitate to ask for advice and help from Kees friends or from your veterinarian, especially if both you and your dog are first-timers at this puppy birthing adventure.

Prepare well in advance for the birth time by obtaining all the necessary items. You will need a heating pad and a temporary-care box lined with soft cloth. Here you will place early arrivals while their siblings are being born. You will also need some heavy surgical thread (dental floss will work) and some sharp safety scissors to tie off and cut the umbilical cords. You will also need some soft, absorbent towels to dry off the newborn puppies. Have an action plan on what to do if a problem arises. Does the veterinarian come to you or do you go to the vet office? Have resources telephone numbers near the phone, just in case.

Whelping

As the puppies emerge, your mother Kees will usually pull away the sac encasing each puppy and bite through the umbilical cord. If she fails to do this, it becomes your job. Carefully tie off and cut each puppy's cord. The dam will usually lick off and clean up each pup and nuzzle it into nursing position. If you assist in any of these duties,

move slowly and try not to excite the bitch or divert her from her pressing maternal duties.

Each birth should be followed by the afterbirth, which the bitch will normally eat. You should be certain that each birth is followed by an expelled amount of afterbirth. If you suspect that any afterbirth has remained inside your Kees female, call your veterinarian.

If the first pups are born much earlier than the later ones, keep the early babies warm on the heating pad in the cloth-lined box. You must help the puppies avoid being chilled until the mother can devote her full attention to keeping all of them comfortably warm.

Care of the Puppies

Your Kees bitch will normally be a very good mother. Her attention to her puppies for the first six weeks of their lives will usually get them off to a great start. Her milk will help give the pups resistance to some of the more common puppy maladies. It will also give them the very best nourishment during the critical early hours and early days.

After your pups reach the age of six weeks they will need the first of a series of immunizations from your veterinarian. Always maintain close communication with your dog's doctor, who can help you recognize or preferably avoid health problems with your bitch and her puppies.

As in other areas of dog care, consistency is important for both mother and offspring. During the first few weeks, the puppies will need an even environment with a temperature range of 80° to 90°F (27°–32°C). Very young Kees, like other young puppies, cannot tolerate cold temperatures, drafts, or extreme swings in temperature. While the mother dog will do what she can to keep them warm, she has to be away from the pups occasionally. Chills can bring on serious problems in very young pups; avoid them.

The puppies will be better able to handle temperature differences after they are five or six weeks old. Their systems by that time will be better developed, making adjustment somewhat easier. In keeping your pups warm always be safety conscious, with heat sources neither too close nor too far from the whelping box. Also keep wires, heating pads, and other electrical devices away from curious (and chewing) puppies.

Your Kees bitch will usually provide all the care the puppies will need for their first few weeks of life. She will feed them, clean them, and even help keep the whelping box clean. She provides warmth and the first lessons in life for the rapidly growing puppies.

Your tasks up to this point have been preparatory. You have kept the female in good health and free from diseases and parasites. You have seen to her changing nutritional needs. You have provided a warm, dry, safe place for the whelping to take place, away from undue noise and commotion that could stress the mother dog. You have seen that the puppies' sire was the best possible and that he was free from inheritable conditions. You have served as a "paw holder" and perhaps as a midwife and have seen that the bitch and pups get regular veterinary care.

If for some reason your bitch is unable to care for her puppies, you may find yourself in the role of surrogate mother. In full consultation with your veterinarian you will need a mother's milk substitute (often called a milk replacer) for bottle feeding the puppies. This becomes quite a job. Hungry little Kees puppies will require feeding about every four hours for the first few weeks of their lives. They will vocalize loudly with whimpers and squeals to let you know they are hungry. Their protestations will generally cease when their little bellies are full. An advantage in hand feeding is the close bonding the puppies will have with their surrogate mother and the early socialization to humans in general.

Weaning the pups at the appropriate time is important for them and their mother. Gradually shifting the youngsters from mother's milk to a more solid diet is your job, beginning at about four to five weeks of age. As with feeding your adult dog, don't stint on the quality of the puppy food. Slowly introduce the pups to moistened small pieces of good-quality puppy food. If you have been feeding such a food to the mother during pregnancy and whelping, this should suffice for the pups. Add some warm water to the puppies' early sampling of dry puppy food, and then gradually cut back on the water as the puppies mature and adjust to the dry food.

One way to introduce puppy food to young puppies is to hold small bits of warm, moist (but not soggy) food in your fingers. The food will have an enticing smell and the puppies will want to lick your fingers and the food. When you do begin to feed them dry food, get a flat-bottomed pan that will allow all pups to eat but which will be hard to upset. Don't feed them in the whelping box. Have some fresh water available nearby at feeding time.

When the puppies turn six weeks old, take them to the veterinarian for their first round of temporary shots. They will also be checked for worms at this time. Even though your puppies have lived only in the whelping box, they can still get roundworms from their mother. The veterinarian will know just what to do both with the shots and with any worms.

When the Kees pups are at this age, it is time to recheck their area for puppy proofing (see page 29). Remember that while you originally puppy-proofed for only one puppy, you are now puppy-proofing for all areas to which the entire litter has access.

Socializing the Puppies

Keeshonden pups are by nature gregarious little creatures, but a structured approach to socialization is not only important, it is fun! Give each puppy some private time with you each day. Be

Raising Quality Keeshonden

Keeshonden are friendly, happy, people-oriented dogs that are adorable as puppies and devoted as adults. A well-bred, well-trained Kees will make a fine pet for a well-prepared household.

playful but tender with the pups, remembering that you want the pup to enjoy, not fear, human contact. Up to this point, you have kept the puppies and their mother out of the limelight of public inspection. Now you can invite some friends and neighbors in to introduce the pups to people other than those in your household. If you are a single person or if your family is all of one gender, you might involve some people of the opposite sex to help your puppies prepare for the big world "out there."

At seven weeks or so, your Keeshond puppies can begin to go to good, well-prepared homes. You will now find yourself in the same position as was the breeder where you got your Kees. If your bitch was of the quality she should have been and you used a top stud dog of comparable pedigree, you may find you have all the puppies "spoken for" even before they are born. You do want to follow the Breeders Code of Ethics (see page 16) and keep a responsible interest in any pups you place for the rest of their lives.

Useful Addresses and Literature

International Kennel Clubs

Keeshond Club of America*
Pat Yagecic
4726 B Grant Avenue
Philadephia, Pennsylvania 19114

*This address may change with the election of new club officers. The current listing can be obtained by contacting the American Kennel Club.

American Kennel Club
51 Madison Avenue
New York, New York 10038

Australian Kennel Club
Royal Show Ground
Ascot Vale
Victoria, Australia

Canadian Kennel Club
2150 Bloor Street West
Toronto, Ontario M6540

The Kennel Club
1-4 Clargis Street
Picadilly
London, W7Y 8AB
England

New Zealand Kennel Club
P.O. Box 523
Wellington, 1
New Zealand

Information and Printed Material

American Boarding Kennel Association
4575 Galley Road, Suite 400 A
Colorado Springs, Colorado 80915
(Publishes lists of approved boarding
kennels.)

American Society for the Prevention of Cruelty
to Animals (ASPCA)
441 East 92nd Street
New York, New York 10128

American Veterinary Medical Association
930 North Meacham Road
Schaumberg, Illinois 60173

Gaines TWT
P.O. Box 8172
Kankakee, Illinois 60901
(Publishes *Touring with Bowser*, a
directory of hotels and motels that
accommodate guests with dogs.)

Humane Society of the United States
2100 L Street NW
Washington, DC 20037

Books

In addition to the most recent edition of the official publication of the American Kennel Club, *The Complete Dog Book,* published by Howell House, Inc., New York, other suggestions include:

Alderton, David, *The Dog Care Manual,* Barron's Educational Series, Inc., Hauppauge, New York, 1986

Baer, Ted, *Communicating with Your Dog,* Barron's Educational Series, Inc., Hauppauge, New York, 1989

___, *How to Teach Your Old Dog New Tricks,* Barron's Educational Series, Inc., Hauppauge, New York, 1991

Useful Addresses and Literature

Frye, Fredric, *First Aid For Your Dog,* Barron's Educational Series, Inc., Hauppauge, New York, 1987

Klever, Ulrich, *The Complete Book of Dog Care,* Barron's Educational Series, Inc., Hauppauge, New York, 1989

——, *Dogs: A Mini Fact Finder,* Barron's Educational Series, Inc., Hauppauge, New York, 1990

Pinney, Chris C., *Guide to Home Pet Grooming,* Barron's Educational Series, Inc., Hauppaguge, New York, 1990

Ullmann, Hans, *The New Dog Handbook,* Barron's Educational Series, Inc., Hauppauge, New York, 1984

Wrede, Barbara, *Civilizing Your Puppy,* Barron's Educational Series, Inc., Hauppauge, New York, 1992

Other Keeshond Reading

"Ebenkeeser Stories"
Mae Evans and Donna Ryan
Ruttkay, 140 Gelsinger Road
Reading, Pennsylvania 19608

Index

Page numbers in **boldface** indicate color photos.

Index